GALÁPAGOS ISLANDS TRAVEL GUIDE

Discover Amazing Wildlife, Explore Underwater Wonders, and Plan Your Perfect Trip

Fred Tovar

Copyright © 2024 Fred Tovar

All rights reserved. No part of this book may be reproduced or transmitted in any form or by any means, electronic or mechanical, including photocopying, recording, or by any information storage and retrieval system, without written permission from the publisher, except in the case of brief quotations embodied in critical articles or reviews.

Disclaimer:

The authors and publisher have made every effort to ensure the accuracy of the information in this book. However, they are not responsible for any errors or omissions, and they disclaim any liability for any damages or losses arising from the use of the information contained herein.

QUICK NOTE

Hey! Before you start reading this guide, there are a few things I need to share with you.

First off, this is the first edition of our guide. We've worked really hard on it, but we know it can get better. Please inform us by leaving a review if you have identified any areas for improvement! Your feedback will help us make future versions even more awesome.

Second, thank you for choosing our travel guide! We are excited to enhance your travel experience with a special bonus: **printable travel journal pages.** These pages are designed to help you document your journey, capture memorable moments, and keep track of your adventures.
To access your printable travel journal pages, simply click on the link or scan the QR code provided on page **94** of this e-book.

Finally, if you enjoy the guide or even feel we could have done something better, do take a moment to leave a review on Amazon. It will help us improve as well as assist other travelers.
Happy travels and enjoyable journaling!

Table of Contents

Planning Your Trip

When to Go	8
Getting There and Around	10
Travel Itinerary	12
Galapagos Travel Cost	18
Tips for Travelers	21
Tourist Information Centers	24

Exploring the Islands

Santa Cruz and Nearby Islands	26
PUERTO AYORA	28
SANTA CRUZ HIGHLANDS	38
SANTA CRUZ ISLANDS	41
San Cristóbal	44
PUERTO BAQUERIZO MORENO	45
OFF THE COAST	57
SAN CRISTÓBAL HIGHLANDS	59
Isabela	62
PUERTO VILLAMIL	64
Around PUERTO VILLAMIL	75
ISABELA HIGHLANDS	78
NORTHERN AND WESTERN ISABELA ISLAND	80
Floreana	82
PUERTO VELASCO IBARRA	83
Highlands of Floreana	89
SURROUNDING ISLETS	91

WELCOME TO GALÁPAGOS ISLANDS

The Galápagos Islands exceed every expectation and offer one of the most extraordinary wildlife experiences on earth. Animals here are unusually unafraid of humans, a result of the absence of natural predators. Unlike most places, you are watched by the wildlife as much as you watch them. With the exception of fish, which are prey for many species, the creatures are either indifferent or curious about visitors. Bird enthusiasts find paradise here—no need for early mornings or binoculars. Birds flaunt their behaviors: male frigates puff out their bright red chests, albatrosses perform their unique clacking courtship dance, and pelicans dramatically dive for their meals. The islands leave a lasting impact, as they did on Charles Darwin, whose observations in 1835 led to his theory of evolution. Isolated and shielded by harsh volcanic landscapes, the Galápagos avoided colonization and destruction for centuries. With the South American coast far to the east and only the vast Pacific Ocean stretching westward, they remained hidden from the world for much of history.

Today, the Galápagos serve as a snapshot of life before human interference, but also as a cautionary tale of the damage we can cause. The impact of human activity is clear—many species have been hunted or nearly wiped out by invasive species. Despite being removed from UNESCO's List of World Heritage in Danger in 2010, the islands still face challenges from illegal fishing, pollution, invasive species, and the pressures of tourism and population growth. Conservation efforts continue, aiming to restore the delicate ecological balance. By visiting with care, you can witness the fragile beauty of nature and leave with a renewed sense of its wonder and importance.

PLANNING YOUR TRIP

- Santa Cruz Island
- San Cristobal
- Isabela
- Floreana Island

Isla Isabela

Puerto Ayora

Puerto Baquerizo Moreno

Puerto Villamil

WHEN TO GO

The ideal period to explore the Galápagos Islands is from **December** to **May**. These months offer pleasant conditions for hiking and observing wildlife, with temperatures ranging between the low 70s and mid-80s. While short showers are common during this time, sunny days dominate, making it a favorable season. From June to November, the Humboldt Current brings cooler temperatures and nutrient-rich waters that attract unique marine life and birds, such as the albatross, which can only be seen on Española Island from April to December. Galápagos penguins migrate from Isabela and Fernandina to central islands like Bartholomew in August. During this season, expect longer rains, stronger winds, and choppier seas, making the waters more challenging for travel.

December to May
Between December and May, visitors enjoy warmer temperatures, with water averaging 76°F and air temperatures ranging from the low 70s to mid-80s. The calm seas and mild weather provide ideal conditions for wildlife enthusiasts to witness animals in their natural habitats.
Birds engage in mating rituals, and from March to May, baby sea lions and sea turtles are a common sight along the shores. Snorkeling is a popular activity during this period, as the clear waters reveal vibrant marine life. Spring brings colorful blooms across the islands, making hikes visually rewarding. However, due to the popularity of the Galápagos from mid-December to mid-January, it's essential to book flights, cruises, and accommodations several months in advance to ensure availability.

June to November
From June to November, the Humboldt Current lowers temperatures to the high 60s and low 80s, creating perfect conditions for underwater activities such as snorkeling and scuba diving. The nutrient-rich waters attract a variety of marine species, while the shores come alive with the mating displays of blue-footed boobies. This period also sees nesting activity from flightless cormorants and Galápagos

penguins. However, the increased rainfall (locally known as garua) and rough seas can make the journey more difficult, especially in August when the water temperature dips to around 70°F. Tourists flock to the islands from mid-June to early September, so it is advisable to book early. Bringing seasickness medication is recommended, even for those who typically don't experience motion sickness, due to the rougher conditions during this time.

To protect this delicate ecosystem, strict regulations control visitor numbers, activity lengths, and site access. Booking in advance is crucial to securing a spot during your preferred travel dates, and staying mindful of environmental guidelines helps preserve the Galápagos for future generations.

Galápagos National Park, Ecuador

GETTING THERE AND AROUND

Entry Requirements for the Galápagos Islands
Before visiting the Galápagos, travelers must secure a $20 transit control card at their departure airport, either in Quito or Guayaquil. This card ensures visitor numbers are regulated to protect the islands. Upon landing, a mandatory $100 national park entrance fee is required, payable in cash. This fee helps maintain the delicate ecosystem. For those holding a student or cultural visa, the fee is reduced to $25, while Ecuadorian citizens pay only $6.

Flights to the Galápagos Islands
Given the Galápagos Islands' remote location, about 600 miles from the Ecuadorian mainland, the only way to access them is by air. No direct international flights go to the islands, so travelers must first fly into Ecuador. There are two main options for international flights: either Quito, the capital city located in the Andes, or Guayaquil, the coastal commercial hub. Once in Ecuador, connecting flights to the Galápagos can be arranged. It's important to note that no boats or cruises operate direct routes from Ecuador's ports to the Galápagos.

Booking a Tour to the Galápagos Islands
When booking a Galápagos tour, it's important to consider that costs generally increase the farther you are from the islands. Cruises, land tours, and diving tours can be organized through agencies in your home country or in Ecuador. If booking from abroad, expect to pay a deposit of around $200 per person via wire transfer or Western Union, as credit card payments are typically not accepted by phone or online. Travel agencies in Quito and Guayaquil frequently advertise tour packages, so shopping around can be worthwhile. While last-minute deals might offer savings of up to 50%, they also come with the risk of being unable to secure a spot. Some budget-conscious travelers even fly to the Galápagos and stay in a cheap hotel while waiting for a last-minute cruise deal, although this

strategy doesn't guarantee savings.

Tours generally last at least five days, but a seven or eight-day trip is recommended, as it takes nearly half a day to reach and depart the islands. When booking a tour, it's essential to inquire about your guide's qualifications and language proficiency.

Tour Operators:

- Angermeyer Cruises/Andando Tours: P.O. Box 17210088, Mariana de Jesús E7-113 at Pradera, Quito, tel. 2/323-7330, www.visitGalápagos.travel
- Lindblad Expeditions: www.expeditions.com
- Ecoventura: www.ecoventura.com
- Silversea: www.silversea.com

Land Tours in the Galápagos

For those seeking a more affordable or flexible experience, land tours are becoming increasingly popular. Ideal for budget travelers, independent explorers, and those prone to seasickness, land tours allow you to stay in a hotel on one of the four inhabited islands. Day trips to explore the islands' unique landscapes and wildlife can be taken, with transportation between the islands provided by speedboat. This option is also appealing for those who wish to scuba dive and spend more time exploring on land.

Land Tour Operators:

- Backroads: www.backroads.com
- G Adventures: www.gadventures.com
- Pikaia Lodge: www.pikaialodgegalapagos.com
- ROW Adventures: www.rowadventures.com

Frigatebirds - Galápagos Islands

TRAVEL ITINERARY

Day 1: Arrival and Exploration of Puerto Baquerizo Moreno

Upon arriving at San Cristóbal's airport on the 10 a.m. flight, take a taxi to your hotel and settle in. Start your day with a leisurely walk along Puerto Baquerizo Moreno's Malecón, where sea lions bask on the beach, providing a picturesque introduction to the island. Head to the San Cristóbal Interpretation Center to get a deeper understanding of the island's culture and history, followed by a hike up Cerro Tijeretas Hill for sweeping views of the turquoise waters below. If you're feeling adventurous, continue to Playa Baquerizo for a hike or swim alongside playful sea lions at Muelle Tijeretas dock. Enjoy lunch at one of the Malecón's many restaurants, offering a chance to refuel before booking a 360 Tour with Galapagos Eco-Fishing for the next day. In the afternoon, embark on a Highlands Tour with a taxi to visit El Junco Crater, the giant tortoises at the Tortoise Center, and the scenic Puerto Chino Beach. Return to town before sunset, freshen up at your hotel, and enjoy a relaxing dinner on the Malecón.

Day 2: Snorkeling and Adventure

Start your day early by heading to Galapagos Eco-Fishing for your 360 Tour. Begin at Leon Dormido, also known as Kicker Rock, where you'll have a good chance of spotting hammerhead sharks while snorkeling in the clear waters. The tour will also take you to stunning spots like Bahia Rosa Blanca Beach, where you can snorkel in a lagoon teeming with rays and sea turtles. If you're lucky, you might even catch some fresh tuna and enjoy sashimi right on the boat. After a day filled with adventure, return to town for a relaxing dinner, and perhaps a peaceful evening walk around Puerto Baquerizo Moreno before turning in for the night.

Day 3: Diving or Beach Day

For diving enthusiasts, Day 3 offers the chance to dive at Kicker Rock, one of the most iconic dive spots in the Galápagos. If diving isn't your preference, consider visiting Española Island, renowned for its unique wildlife, including pink and green iguanas and the waved albatross. Alternatively, for those on a budget, a trip to La Loberia Beach by taxi, foot, or bicycle offers the opportunity to swim or surf with sea lions in a serene setting. As the day winds down, relax at Playa Mann or Punta Carola Beach, both of which are conveniently located near the town center and provide excellent spots for surfing or simply unwinding by the water.

Day 4: Departure

On your final morning, make time for some last-minute souvenir shopping or visit one of the nearby beaches before your flight, which departs around 1 p.m. Be sure to leave enough time for the necessary airport procedures and controls to ensure a smooth departure from San Cristóbal.

5-day Galapagos Itinerary

Day 1: Arriving in San Cristobal and Exploring Puerto Baquerizo Moreno

Upon landing at San Cristóbal's airport on the 10 a.m. flight, take a taxi to your hotel and settle in. Start your exploration with a walk along Puerto Baquerizo Moreno's Malecón, where sea lions often relax on the beach, giving you a true Galapagos welcome. Afterward, visit San Cristóbal's Interpretation Center to learn about the island's history and culture. For panoramic views, hike up Cerro Tijeretas Hill and take in the stunning turquoise waters below. If you're feeling adventurous, continue to Playa Baquerizo for a hike, or swim with baby sea lions at Muelle Tijeretas dock. Enjoy lunch at one of the restaurants along the Malecón. Later in the day, book a 360 Tour with Galapagos Eco-Fishing for the following day. In the afternoon, take a Highlands Tour by taxi to visit El Junco Crater, the Tortoise Center, and Puerto Chino Beach. Return to town before sunset, freshen up, and have dinner back on the Malecón.

Day 2: Snorkeling and Touring with Galapagos Eco-Fishing

Begin your day early with a visit to the Galapagos Eco-Fishing store for your pre-booked 360 Tour. Opt for the tour that first takes you to Leon Dormido, also known as Kicker Rock, to maximize your chances of seeing hammerhead sharks while snorkeling. The tour continues to picturesque beaches like Bahia Rosa Blanca, where you can snorkel in a massive lagoon filled with rays and sea turtles. If you're lucky, you might catch fresh tuna and enjoy sashimi on the boat. After a day of adventure, return to town for a quiet dinner and perhaps a peaceful evening stroll around Puerto Baquerizo Moreno before calling it a night.

Day 3: Diving or Exploring Española Island

For those who enjoy diving, today is perfect for a Kicker Rock Dive, one of the most renowned spots in the Galapagos. If diving isn't your thing, consider a visit to Española Island, home to some of the archipelago's most unique wildlife, including pink and green iguanas and the waved albatross. Alternatively, for a more budget-friendly option, head to La Loberia Beach by taxi, on foot, or by bicycle, where you can swim with sea lions or surf. In the evening, wind down at Playa Mann or Punta Carola Beach, both of which are conveniently located near the town center and offer great spots for surfing or simply relaxing.

Day 4: Journey to Santa Cruz and Exploration

Catch the 7 a.m. speedboat to Santa Cruz Island, arriving around 9:30 - 10 a.m. Once you've dropped off your bags at your hotel in Puerto Ayora, head to the docks and take a taxi-boat to Las Grietas, a popular snorkeling spot. After snorkeling, return to Puerto Ayora, grab a quick sandwich or snack for lunch, and make your way to the renowned Tortuga Bay Beach. Spend a few hours snorkeling and relaxing at this beautiful beach before deciding whether to hike back to town or stay a bit longer. If you return by 2 p.m., you can embark on a Highlands Tour of Santa Cruz, where a taxi can take you to the Lava Tunnels, Los Gemelos, and the Giant Tortoise Ranch. After a full day, unwind with a stroll around town, do some shopping, have a craft beer, or enjoy dinner in the vibrant town of Puerto Ayora.

Day 5: Departure from the Galapagos

If you're an early riser, start your final day with a quick visit to the Charles Darwin Research Station for an educational session on conservation efforts. Afterward, pack your bags, enjoy breakfast, and complete your checkout before making your way to the airport. If you missed any shopping in Puerto Ayora, you'll find a variety of shops at the airport to pick up any last-minute souvenirs. Be sure to allow plenty of time to get through airport security and procedures before your departure.

7-day Galapagos Itinerary

Day 1: Arrival and Exploration of San Cristobal

After arriving at San Cristobal's airport on the 10 a.m. flight, take a taxi to your hotel and settle in. Begin your adventure by walking along the Malecón in Puerto Baquerizo Moreno, where sea lions often rest on the beach, offering an authentic Galapagos experience. Head to San Cristobal's Interpretation Center for a brief introduction to the island's culture and history. Next, hike up Cerro Tijeretas Hill for breathtaking views of the turquoise waters below. For more outdoor activities, hike to Playa Baquerizo Beach or swim with baby sea lions at Muelle Tijeretas dock. Afterward, have lunch at one of the restaurants along the Malecón. Book a 360 Tour with Galapagos Eco-Fishing for the next day and spend the afternoon on a Highlands Tour by taxi, visiting El Junco Crater, the Giant Tortoise Center, and Puerto Chino Beach. Return to town before sunset, freshen up at the hotel, and enjoy dinner along the Malecón.

Day 2: Snorkeling and Beach Exploration

Start your day early at the Galapagos Eco-Fishing store to begin your tour. Choose the itinerary that starts at Leon Dormido (Kicker Rock) to increase your chances of spotting hammerhead sharks while snorkeling. The tour includes visits to pristine beaches like Bahia Rosa Blanca, where you can snorkel in a large lagoon with rays and giant turtles. If you're lucky, you might even catch fresh tuna and enjoy sashimi on the boat. After returning to town, enjoy a peaceful dinner and consider strolling through the quiet streets of Puerto Baquerizo Moreno.

Day 3: Travel to Santa Cruz and Island Exploration

Catch the 7 a.m. speedboat to Santa Cruz Island, arriving in Puerto Ayora by 9:30 – 10 a.m. After dropping off your luggage at the hotel, head to the docks for a taxi-boat ride to Las Grietas, where you can snorkel in the crystal-clear waters. Return to Puerto Ayora for lunch along the Malecón and then visit the Charles Darwin Research Station to see giant tortoises and learn about conservation efforts. In the afternoon, spend a few hours at Tortuga Bay Beach, one of the most beautiful spots on Santa Cruz. After relaxing at the beach, hike back to town and take a leisurely stroll, do some shopping, and enjoy a craft beer or dinner in Puerto Ayora, the archipelago's most vibrant town.

Day 4: Highlands Tour and Isabela Island Transfer

After breakfast, embark on the Highlands Tour of Santa Cruz, visiting the Lava Tunnels, Los Gemelos twin craters, and a Giant Tortoise Ranch. Once you've completed the tour, enjoy a satisfying lunch at one of the Malecón's restaurants. In the afternoon, catch the 2 p.m. ferry to Puerto Villamil on Isabela Island. After checking in and unpacking at your hotel, relax and book a Sierra Negra Volcano Tour for the following day, a Los Tuneles Tour for Day 6, and the 6 a.m. speedboat back to Santa Cruz for Day 7. End the evening with dinner at a local restaurant before heading back to your hotel to rest.

Day 5: Hiking Sierra Negra and Snorkeling

Start early with the Sierra Negra Volcano hike, where you can enjoy stunning views and learn about the island's volcanic history. Afterward, head to Concha de Perla Lagoon for snorkeling, where you can spot marine iguanas, sea turtles, and rays. If you prefer not to snorkel, visit the nearby Flamingo Lagoon before sunset. Enjoy a fresh seafood dinner at a beachside restaurant and then return to your hotel for some much-needed rest.

Day 6: Los Tuneles Snorkeling Adventure

Today's highlight is the Los Tuneles Tour, widely regarded as one of the best snorkeling experiences in the Galapagos. You'll have the chance to see penguins, reef sharks, sea turtles, and rays swimming through underwater lava tunnels. On the surface, keep an eye out for blue-footed boobies and admire the unique landscape. Lunch will be served on the boat during the tour. Afterward, explore anything you may have missed the previous day, such as the Flamingo Lagoon or Concha de Perla Lagoon. Spend your last night on the island enjoying a relaxing dinner by the sea.

Day 7: Departure from Isabela Island

Make sure to book a flight departing at 1 p.m. to allow time for this itinerary. Take the 6 a.m. speedboat back to Santa Cruz, arriving around 9 a.m. Upon arrival, take a stroll along Puerto Ayora's Malecón, where you can visit the Fish Market and stop by some souvenir shops. Finally, take a taxi to Itabaca Channel, cross by taxi-boat, and board a bus to the airport. Be sure to allow plenty of time to pass through airport controls and procedures before your flight departure.

Galapagos Penguin on Bartolomé Island

GALAPAGOS TRAVEL COST

Flight cost
When planning a trip to the Galapagos Islands, expect to pay between $500 and $550 per person for flights. Booking early and being flexible with your travel dates can help reduce costs. Additionally, you'll need to budget for the $20 Transit Control Card, which is required to enter the islands. If booking through GreenGo Travel, ensure your flight aligns with their terms, as some cruises may impose fees if airfare isn't arranged through them.

Park Fees and Conservation Costs
Upon arrival, you'll be required to pay a Galapagos National Park entrance fee, which currently stands at $100 but will increase to $200 starting August 1, 2024. This mandatory fee contributes to the conservation of the islands' natural habitats. Though this adds to your expenses, it supports vital ecological preservation efforts and helps maintain the infrastructure on the islands.

Budget-Friendly Accommodations options
For travelers seeking affordable lodging, the inhabited islands of the Galapagos, such as Santa Cruz and San Cristobal, offer budget accommodations ranging from $30 to $40 per night for a double room. These options provide a simple yet comfortable stay, allowing visitors to experience the islands without overspending. Staying in local guesthouses also offers a closer connection to island life.

Mid-Range and Luxury accommodation Options
For those desiring more comfort, mid-range to luxury accommodations are also available, with nightly rates ranging from $81 to $194. These accommodations typically offer extra amenities and a relaxing atmosphere, perfect after a day of exploring the islands. Luxury travelers can expect additional services and larger, more comfortable spaces.

Cost of Outdoor Activities

A significant portion of your budget will go toward tours and activities, essential for immersing yourself in the unique wildlife and scenery of the Galapagos. Land-based tours cost around $220 per person, while sea-based excursions range from $150 to $250. Popular activities include snorkeling with sea lions, visiting the Charles Darwin Research Station, and hiking Sierra Negra Volcano. Choosing a few key tours that align with your interests will maximize your experience without unnecessary expenses.

Exploring the Galapagos by land is an exciting way to discover its volcanic landscapes and wildlife. Depending on the level of service, land-based activities may cost between $340 and $515 per day. To balance the budget, consider mixing in free or low-cost experiences like visiting iconic sites on Santa Cruz Island or snorkeling at Isabela's Concha de la Perla.

For water enthusiasts, sea tours are a must. Scuba diving around Santa Cruz costs approximately $250 per day, including equipment and meals. This investment provides access to extraordinary underwater encounters, such as swimming alongside sea turtles and hammerhead sharks near North Seymour Island, creating unforgettable memories.

Dining and accommodation in the Galapagos

Dining and daily expenses in the Galapagos are generally higher due to the islands' remote location, which drives up prices. Meals cost an average of $40 to $45 per day, but dining at local eateries can reduce this. Meals at local restaurants typically cost around $13, offering both authentic flavors and savings.

Daily Costs to Consider

On top of meals, other expenses may arise, including fees for internet access, which can be slow, taxi fares, and beverages. A typical drink costs between $10 and $15, and it's common to tip around $13 per day. Factoring in these extras will help keep your budget on track during your stay.

When deciding how to explore the Galapagos, you'll need to choose between a cruise or a land-based tour. A 5-day cruise averages $3,200 per person, while a land tour costs around $2,500. Cruises provide an all-inclusive experience with meals and excursions, while land tours allow for more flexibility in dining and activities.

Costs of Galapagos cruises

Cruises range from $1,500 for budget options to over $7,000 for luxury experiences. The cost per day can vary from $550 to $699 depending on the level of service. Booking during the low season can result in discounts of 10-50%. For those looking to stretch their dollars, last-minute deals can offer significant savings.

Land tours present a cost-effective alternative to cruises. A 4-day land tour starts at $1,000 for budget travelers, while luxury land-based tours cost around $3,500. Land tours offer a wider variety of dining choices and the flexibility to pick and choose excursions, making them a versatile option.

Saving Money Tips

Booking in advance is key to securing lower prices. Keep an eye out for last-minute cruise offers, which can slash prices by 50%. Day tours also offer an affordable way to experience the islands without the high costs of a multi-day cruise.

Choosing the Best Time to Visit

Timing your trip during the off-peak season can save up to $500 per person on international flights and provide a less crowded experience. Traveling during less popular periods can also lead to quieter attractions, making the trip more enjoyable.

Booking Tips and Tour Discounts

To maximize your budget, consider negotiating for discounts with local agencies like GreenGo Travel. Last-minute cruises can sometimes drop to $200 per day, offering an all-inclusive package at a lower cost. By focusing on activities that are most meaningful to you, you can manage your expenses while fully enjoying the islands.

Seal Pup. Galápagos Islands

TIPS FOR TRAVELERS

Ensure You Have $120 in Cash for National Park Fees
To enter the Galápagos Islands, you will need to pay a $20 transit card fee in cash at either the Quito or Guayaquil airports. This card acts as your entry visa for the islands. Upon arrival in the Galápagos, an additional $100 national park fee is required, also paid in cash. These fees contribute to the conservation efforts of the Galápagos' delicate ecosystems, which are under constant monitoring by park authorities. Typically, tours do not cover these fees, so it's best to be prepared to handle them on-site.

Don't Forget Ample Sun Protection
Since the Galápagos Islands sit directly on the equator, the sun's intensity can be overwhelming no matter the season. Whether you're visiting during the cooler, misty dry season or the warmer, wetter season, the sun's rays remain strong, making it easy to get sunburned. Be sure to bring high-SPF sunscreen, a wide-brimmed hat, UV-protective sunglasses, and light, long-sleeved clothing to stay protected throughout your trip. Even if the skies are overcast, UV exposure remains high in this region.

Prepare for Water Activities
The Galápagos Islands offer as much excitement in the water as they do on land. Depending on the type of tour you select, you could participate in activities such as swimming, snorkeling, kayaking, paddleboarding, or even diving. Higher-end tours tend to offer a greater variety of these experiences. Although many tours include equipment such as wetsuits and snorkels, it's wise to double-check what is provided before you leave. If you are joining a diving tour, bringing your own gear can improve your experience. It's recommended to pack several bathing suits, as water-based activities might take up a significant portion of your day.

Expect Hot Days and Cooler Nights
Galápagos weather is relatively stable year-round due to its proximity to the equator, but temperatures do fluctuate between day and night. During the day, it tends to be hot, so

lightweight clothing is ideal. However, the evenings can get cooler, so packing a few sweaters or jackets will help you stay comfortable as temperatures dip after sunset.

Plan Your Trip Well in Advance
A trip to the Galápagos is often considered a once-in-a-lifetime experience, so planning well in advance is crucial. Many people start organizing their trip at least a year beforehand to secure their ideal tour and accommodations. Early planning also helps avoid disappointment as tour spots fill up quickly. In addition, travel insurance is highly recommended in case unforeseen circumstances affect your trip.

Bring Your Best Camera
The Galápagos Islands are a photographer's paradise, with an abundance of wildlife and stunning landscapes. You'll likely take hundreds of photos daily, with a few being worthy of a nature magazine. Be sure to bring your best camera, and if you own an underwater camera, pack it too. There's a good chance you'll be swimming alongside sea turtles, penguins, sharks, and a variety of colorful fish, making underwater photography an unforgettable part of your experience.

Expect Limited Connectivity
Cell service and WiFi are scarce in the Galápagos, particularly when you're outside of the main towns. Even in the towns, the connection is satellite-based and often slow. Use this as an opportunity to disconnect and immerse yourself in the natural beauty of the islands. Let go of daily stresses and enjoy the environment, as the rest of the world can wait until you return.

Prepare for a Busy Schedule
A typical Galápagos itinerary is packed with activities from early morning until late at night. There's a lot to see and do, so it's best to make the most of each day. While the busy schedule may leave you with little time to rest, the experiences are worth the effort. It's a good idea to plan a rest day after your trip to recover from the whirlwind of adventures.

Stay Present
When visiting the Galápagos, take the time to fully engage with your surroundings. Whether you're observing wildlife, walking through the islands, or sharing moments with loved ones, staying present will enhance your experience and deepen your appreciation for the natural

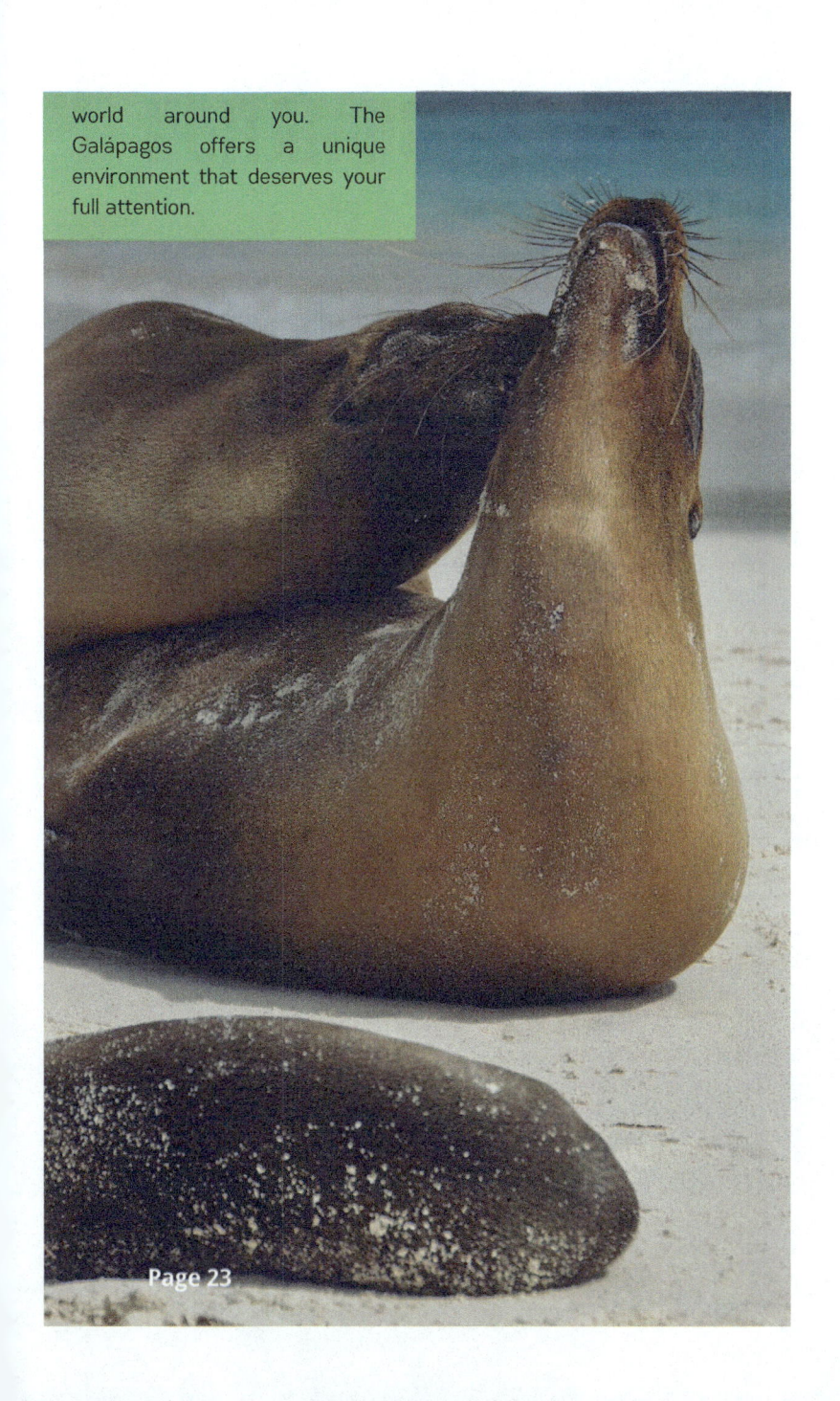

world around you. The Galápagos offers a unique environment that deserves your full attention.

TOURIST INFORMATION CENTERS

For those planning a trip to the Galápagos Islands, it is important to have access to reliable resources and information about the region. The International Galápagos Tour Operators Association offers comprehensive details regarding tour options, travel guidelines, and sustainability efforts at www.igtoa.org. If you are interested in learning about the unique wildlife, plant life, and the ongoing conservation work in the islands, the Charles Darwin Foundation provides in-depth knowledge through their website at www.darwinfoundation.org. Another valuable resource is the Galápagos Conservation Trust, which focuses on protecting the natural environment of the Galápagos; more information can be found at www.galapagosconservation.org.uk. These websites will provide useful insights and guidance to help you plan your journey responsibly and sustainably.

Health and Emergency Contacts

In case of any emergency while visiting the Galápagos Islands, the primary contact number for urgent assistance is 911. This general emergency number will connect you to ambulance services, fire departments, or the police. Additionally, you can dial 131 directly for an ambulance, 102 for fire emergencies, and 101 for the police. Always keep these numbers accessible during your stay to ensure a prompt response in case of any situation that requires immediate attention.

EXPLORING THE ISLANDS

SANTA CRUZ AND NEARBY ISLANDS

Santa Cruz Island is the main hub of the Galápagos, serving as the perfect starting point for day trips to nearby islands and securing last-minute tour deals. The island's attractions are accessible without the need for guided tours, offering flexibility to independent travelers. Puerto Ayora, the island's primary town, offers the broadest range of accommodations and dining, making it a convenient base for exploring the surrounding central islands.

A visit to the Charles Darwin Research Station, located on the outskirts of Puerto Ayora, provides a close-up view of the island's famous giant tortoises and an insight into conservation efforts. A 45-minute walk west of town leads to Tortuga Bay, a stunning stretch of sand ideal for relaxing. Another nearby attraction, Las Grietas, is a natural formation in the lava rocks, where visitors can enjoy a cool, refreshing swim in its brackish waters, just a short hike from Puerto Ayora.

The lush highlands of Santa Cruz offer a unique contrast to the coastal areas and make for an intriguing day trip. Two impressive craters, known as Los Gemelos, are home to abundant birdlife, making it a popular spot for bird watchers. Further east, near Bellavista, visitors can explore the remarkable lava tunnels formed from ancient molten lava flows. The peaceful Playa Garrapatero beach also lies in this region, perfect for a quiet escape. However, the main attraction in the highlands is undoubtedly the giant tortoise reserves, where these iconic creatures can be seen roaming in their natural habitat.

Island Day Tours and Diving Opportunities
Several smaller islands surrounding Santa Cruz are accessible via day trips, providing a chance to experience the region's diverse wildlife. Bartolomé Island, known for the iconic Pinnacle Rock, is a favorite destination. Trips to Santa Fé

and Plaza Sur offer sightings of land iguanas, while Seymour Norte is known for its nesting frigate birds. For snorkeling enthusiasts, Pinzón Island is a top choice, where the waters are teeming with sharks, sea lions, and turtles. For those interested in exploring further, day tours to the more populated islands of Isabela, San Cristóbal, and Floreana are available, though staying overnight often allows for a deeper experience of these islands.

Santa Cruz also has the most options for diving enthusiasts, with numerous agencies offering trips to some of the best dive spots in the Galápagos. Gordon Rocks is renowned for sightings of schooling hammerhead sharks, and other popular dive sites include Floreana, Seymour Norte, and Daphne. These excursions offer divers the chance to explore the rich underwater life that surrounds the islands.

Galápagos tortoise on Santa Cruz Island

PUERTO AYORA

If you're envisioning Puerto Ayora as a tranquil, remote island retreat, you'll be surprised to find a bustling town with around 18,000 permanent residents and an influx of visitors and temporary workers. The waterfront area is lined with tourist-focused establishments like restaurants, travel agencies, souvenir shops, and hotels. Despite its commercial atmosphere, the town is still charming, offering a scenic bay dotted with yachts and framed by cacti. The illuminated docks at night add to the appeal, and the small fish market near Banco del Pacifico draws the attention of pelicans and sea lions hoping to snag scraps from the day's catch. For independent travelers, Puerto Ayora is a practical base, as it allows easy access to day tours and last-minute cruise options.

However, Puerto Ayora isn't without its downsides. The town can be noisy, with constant traffic and numerous white taxis shuttling visitors around. Just a short walk inland reveals piles of construction debris and unfinished buildings, giving parts of the town a less appealing look. Additionally, the cost of boat day tours continues to rise, making excursions more expensive. The town also faces issues with its water supply and sewage treatment, both of which have long been in need of upgrades. Visitors should avoid drinking the tap water due to its poor quality, which is worse than that of mainland Ecuador. It's also advisable to use bottled water even for basic hygiene tasks like brushing your teeth.

Sights

Charles Darwin Research Station
The Charles Darwin Research Station (Av. Charles Darwin s/n, Puerto Ayora, tel. 05/252-7013 ext. 101, darwinfoundation.org, 7:30am-5pm, free admission) serves as a significant center for conservation. A key feature here is the Fausto Llerena Tortoise Breeding Center, established in the 1960s to protect and raise endangered subspecies. The station has successfully reintroduced thousands of giant tortoises into the wild, particularly from Española Island, where the population

once dwindled to just 14. Visitors can see adult tortoises, tiny hatchlings in protective boxes, and the preserved body of Lonesome George, the last of the Pinta Island tortoises who died in 2012. Although the research buildings are off-limits, the visitor center offers exhibits about Galápagos wildlife, and there's a small beach, Playa de la Estación, just outside the station. It's a short 15-minute walk east of Puerto Ayora, making it easily accessible for independent travelers. If you're visiting multiple islands, you might only need to explore one of the tortoise breeding centers since they share many similarities.

Playa de los Alemanes

Playa de los Alemanes, or German Beach, is a small, easily accessible beach just a short water taxi ride away from Puerto Ayora, costing $0.80 each way. Although not the most scenic or wildlife-rich, it's the closest spot for sunbathing and swimming near town, and it's situated in front of the Finch Bay Eco Hotel, yet open to the public. From the pier, the beach is a five-minute walk past the Angermeyer Waterfront Inn, making it a convenient stop on the way to Las Grietas.

Las Grietas

Las Grietas is a popular swimming spot nestled between steep red rock cliffs, with clear turquoise waters ideal for a relaxing dip. The natural pool stretches further than it initially seems, and adventurers can climb over slippery rocks to reach the quieter second section. If you're up for more exploration, there's even an underwater tunnel for those willing to dive deeper. To get to Las Grietas, take a water taxi ($0.80 each way) across the bay from Puerto Ayora, then follow a well-maintained trail past the Finch Bay Eco Hotel. The swim hole can get crowded, so visiting early in the day or heading to the second section offers a quieter experience.

Tortuga Bay

Tortuga Bay is one of the most beautiful beaches in the Galápagos, located about 45 minutes west of Puerto Ayora on a well-paved path through a cactus forest. The walk, starting from the national park guard post, is peaceful, with finches and other birds to spot along the way. Once you arrive, Playa Brava welcomes surfers with its strong waves, while Playa Mansa, a calmer lagoon further along, offers a serene spot for swimming. Marine iguanas and blue-footed boobies are common here, and if the water is clear, you might see turtles, reef sharks, and rays. The beach closes at 5pm, so it's essential to plan accordingly. There are no facilities, so pack water and snacks, and remember to carry out your trash. For those looking to avoid the walk, boats depart from the dock at 9am and noon, costing $10 each way.

Tours

Highlands Tours

Highlands tours ($45) offer an insightful look into the natural beauty of Santa Cruz Island. These tours typically cover the El Chato Tortoise Reserve, where you can see giant tortoises in their natural habitat, and the nearby lava tunnels and Los Gemelos collapsed craters. Alternatively, you can arrange a taxi tour for about $40, which can be shared among your group for a more private experience.

Bay Tours

Bay tours ($35) are half-day excursions departing at 9am and 2pm daily. These trips take you to La Lobería to see sea lions, snorkel at Punta Estrada, and explore the cliffs where blue-footed boobies nest. The tour includes a stop at Canal del Amor, where white-tipped reef sharks rest in the shallow waters, and concludes at Las Grietas for a refreshing swim. Tour boats are typically small and slow, but some offer glass-bottomed viewing areas for a closer look at marine life. It's recommended to request free fin rentals from your tour agency to enhance your snorkeling experience.

Day Tours

Full-day tours from Puerto Ayora to nearby islands are the most sought-after excursions and come at a higher price ($160-$250). A trip to Seymour Norte offers an opportunity to walk among frigate bird colonies, while Plaza Sur is known for its land iguanas and sea lions. The famous Pinnacle Rock on Bartolomé Island is a highlight, with snorkeling in the bay afterward. Santa Fé tours focus on the endemic land iguanas, with snorkeling included, though a more affordable fishing trip with snorkeling ($120) is also an option. The comfort of the day-tour yachts varies, with luxury options like the Adriana (tel. 99/171-6411, www.adrianagalapagos.com) and Promesa

(Galápagos Daily Tours, Baltra at Tomás de Berlanga, tel. 5/252-7337) offering more amenities, including onboard meals and sunbathing areas. Standard yachts include Española (www.espanolatours.com.ec), Altamar (tel. 5/252-6430, Galápagosaltamartours.com), and Sea Finch (tel. 99/980-3147, www.seafinch.com).

Tour Operators and Agencies

Many tour agencies are conveniently located along Avenida Darwin, making it easy to compare prices and book excursions. Recommended operators include Galápagos Voyager (Darwin at Colón, tel. 5/252-6833, Galápagosvoyages2008@hotmail.com), Moonrise Travel (Darwin, tel. 5/252-6348, www.Galápagosmoonrise.com), We Are the Champions Tours (Darwin, tel. 5/252-6951, www.wearethechampionstours.com), Galapatur (Rodríguez Lara and Genovesa, tel. 5/252-6088), and Galápagos Deep (Indefatigable and Matazarno, tel. 5/252-7045, www.Galápagosdeep.com).

Always ensure you get quotes from multiple agencies to secure the best deal on your desired tour.

Outdoor Adventures in Santa Cruz

Kayaking and Stand-Up Paddleboarding (SUP)

In Santa Cruz, kayaking is a popular activity with rentals available at three key spots: the dock for exploring the bay, Tortuga Bay for paddling among mangroves, and El Garrapatero Beach. Kayaks cost $10 per person. Stand-up paddleboards are also available at Galadventure Tours, where you can rent them for $25 per day. For inquiries, contact Galadventure Tours at 5/252-4119 or visit their website at www.galadventure.com for more information on booking your SUP adventure.

Cycling Through the Highlands

Cycling offers a unique way to explore the highlands of Santa Cruz. You can take a bus or taxi to Bellavista, which is 6 kilometers away, or to Santa Rosa, which is 15 kilometers from Puerto Ayora. From there, enjoy a long downhill ride back into town. Buses to Santa Rosa ($1.50) and Bellavista ($1) depart from Mercado Central, with some buses equipped with bike racks. Be sure to check with the driver as not all buses have this option. The ride includes a protected bike lane, which extends only to Santa Rosa.

Beyond this point, cycling is discouraged due to the lack of a dedicated lane. However, you can take a scenic detour along Guayabillos, a quiet country road lined with farms, eventually looping back to the highway. If you're feeling adventurous, take a detour from Santa Rosa on a bumpy dirt road to El Chato or Rancho Primicias to visit the famous giant tortoises. Keep in mind this route is only advisable in dry weather.

For a different experience, you can bike to El Garrapatero Beach, a 14-kilometer journey from Bellavista. The route is mostly downhill, and it offers a stunning transition from the lush highlands to the dry coastal plains. From Bellavista, it's a 7-kilometer climb to the small town of Cascajo, where you can grab some water and ice cream before descending another 7 kilometers to the beach. Most bike rental shops in Puerto Ayora open at 8 a.m., but it's a good idea to rent your bike the night before if you plan on an early start.

Diving in the Galápagos

The Galápagos Islands are renowned for their incredible diving spots, suitable for divers of all levels. Day tours are a popular choice, with prices ranging from $170 to $200 per person for two dives. Galápagos Sub-Aqua, located on Darwin Street in Puerto Ayora, is one of the most established diving centers with 20 years of experience (tel. 5/252-6350 or 5/252-6633, www.Galapagos-subaqua.com). Another reputable operator is Scuba Iguana, run by the renowned dive master Matías Espinosa (tel. 5/252-6497, www.scubaiguana.com), offering daily dive trips starting at $200 per person. Other respected operators include Academy Bay Diving (tel. 5/252-4164, https://academybaydiving.com) and Nauti Diving (tel. 5/252-7004, www.nautidiving.com).

For experienced divers, Gordon Rocks is a must-see site, famous for its schools of hammerhead sharks. The strong currents make it suitable only for advanced divers with over 30 dives. Other notable sites include Seymour Norte, Mosquera, and Daphne, all within 30 minutes from Ithabaca Channel. Seymour Norte is known for its shark populations, while Mosquera offers calmer waters with plenty of eels. If you're up for a longer boat ride, Beagle Rocks, Bartolomé, and Cousins Rock are 90 minutes from Ithabaca

Channel and offer stunning marine life, including manta rays, seahorses, and Galápagos eels. Floreana also has excellent dive sites such as Champion Island and Punta Cormorant, although dives here can only be arranged via day tours from Puerto Ayora, as there are no local operators on the island.

Each diving operator provides transportation, and in case of emergencies, there is a decompression chamber available at the main hospital in Puerto Ayora.

Shopping in Puerto Ayora

The best place for souvenir shopping in Puerto Ayora is along Avenida Darwin, especially as you head towards the Charles Darwin Research Station. A standout is the vibrant Angelique Gallery, located at the corner of Darwin and Indefatigable. Open from 9am to 1pm and 3pm to 9pm Monday through Saturday, and 3pm to 8pm on Sundays (tel. 5/252-6656), it showcases the creative works of U.K. expat Sarah Darling. Her artistic expression captures the Galápagos in bold colors, with her pieces displayed on mirrors, silk pillows, and scarves. She also offers unique handcrafted jewelry.

Nearby, Galápagos Jewelry is situated at Darwin and Piqueros and at Darwin and Indefatigable (tel. 5/252-6044, www.galapagosjewelry.com). It's open from 9am to 12:30pm and 3pm to 9pm daily, featuring exquisite sterling silver pieces. At the end of the block, Galería Aymara (Darwin and Piqueros, tel. 5/252-6835, www.galeria-aymara.com) opens from 8am to noon and 3pm to 7pm Monday through Saturday, offering Latin American artwork, including pieces from indigenous communities.

Food and Dining Options in Puerto Ayora

Puerto Ayora is known for offering a wide range of dining experiences, from affordable meals to more expensive options. For budget-conscious travelers, $5 **almuerzos** (lunches) are a great deal, with international restaurants lining the malecón.

For coffee and snacks, **OMG Galápagos**, located at Darwin and Piqueros, serves up espresso drinks for $4 (tel. 098/916-9540, 7:30am to 7:30pm Monday to Saturday, and 3pm to 7:30pm Sunday). They source their beans from local highland farms and roast them on-site, offering air-conditioning to accompany their frozen yogurt and snacks. Another treat is **Chocolápagos** at Darwin and Marchena (tel. 096/738-9575, 10am to 5pm Monday to Saturday), which specializes in handmade truffles and offers chocolate-making demonstrations for $15 by reservation.

For local Ecuadorian and seafood fare, **El Descanso del Guia** on Darwin is a favorite among guides (tel. 5/252-6618, 6:30am to 7:30pm daily). Offering set lunches for $5 and entrées priced between $8 and $12, the restaurant serves large portions of chicken, fish, and meat. Another popular choice is **Los Kioskos** along Charles Binford, where locals and tourists flock for fresh seafood, especially the seasonal lobster and langostino. One of the best stalls is Servisabroson (Binford, tel. 5/252-7461), where you can enjoy a fixed-menu lunch for $4, with dinner entrées ranging from $10 to $13.

For international flavors, **Galápagos Deli** (Berlanga and Baltra, open from 7am to 10pm Tuesday to Sunday, $5 to $10) is known for its affordable pizzas, fresh salads, and sandwiches, plus free Wi-Fi. **Il Giardino** (Darwin and Binford, tel. 5/252-6627, www.ilgiardinogalapagos.com.ec) serves Italian specialties from 8:30am to 11:30pm Tuesday to Sunday, with entrées priced between $7 and $14. **The Rock**, another favorite, offers a casual dining experience with a variety of international dishes and drinks (Darwin and Naveda, tel. 5/252-7505, www.therockgalapagos.com, 8:30am to 11pm Tuesday to Sunday, $8 to $18 per entrée).

For fine dining, **Almar,** located in the Red Mangrove Hotel, offers stunning sunset views of the harbor (Darwin, tel. 98/462-7240, http://almargalapagos.com, 7am to 10pm daily). The menu features fresh seafood and international cuisine, with entrées ranging from $15 to $25. Another top-tier option is **Anker Mar** (Binford at Plazas, tel. 05/252-4994, 6pm to 10pm Tuesday to Sunday), offering a farm-to-table menu with specialties like brujo ceviche and roasted octopus. The six-course tasting menu costs $55, while individual entrées range from $18 to $27.

For groceries, **Supermarket Pro-Insular** (Darwin and Malecón) operates daily from 8am to 9pm and is conveniently located near the pier. For a more local experience, visit the **Municipal Market** (Baltra and Calle No 55), which opens daily at 5:30am and sells fresh fruits, vegetables, and eggs. Fresh seafood, including fish, lobster, and langostino, can be found at the fish market on Darwin and Indefatigable, which operates in the mornings and evenings.

Accommodations in Puerto Ayora

Puerto Ayora offers a wide range of accommodations, from budget to luxury. Prices vary, with many cheaper options available if booked directly through email or phone, rather than online platforms.

For budget travelers, **Los Amigos** (Charles Darwin, tel. 05/252-6265, $15 single, $30 double, no breakfast) offers the cheapest rooms in town, with basic amenities. **Hostal Morning Glory** (Darwin and Floreana, tel. 099/680-5789, $20 single, $40 double, breakfast $5) provides colorful rooms around a small garden, making it one of the most charming budget options. **Vista al Mar** (Baltra and Binford, tel. 05/252-4109, $30 single, $50 double) includes bike rental, snorkels, and fins with its centrally located rooms.

Crossman Hostal (Binford and Montalvo, tel. 5/252-6467, www.crossmanhotel.com.ec) offers dorm beds for $20 and private rooms for $30 single and $50 double, with access to a shared kitchen.

In the midrange, **Hostal Flightless Cormorant** (Darwin and 12 de Febrero, tel. 05/252-4343, $30 single, $60 double, breakfast $5) provides comfortable rooms and access to a shared kitchen. Another midrange choice is **Galápagos Native** (Berlanga and 12 de Febrero, tel. 5/252-4730, www.galapagosnative.com.ec), which offers rooms starting at $60, with breakfast included at a nearby café.

For those seeking luxury, Hotel **Silberstein** (Darwin and Los Piqueros, tel./fax 5/252-6277, www.hotelsilberstein.com, $240 double) provides a tropical oasis with a swimming pool and solar-heated water. **The exclusive Red Mangrove Hotel** (Darwin, tel. 593/5252-6564, www.redmangrove.com, $350-370 double) offers rooms nestled within a mangrove forest, with luxury amenities and waterfront views.

Information and Services

For local information, the Cámara de Turismo office (Darwin and 12 de Febrero, tel. 5/252-6206, www.galapagostour.org, 9am-5pm Monday to Friday) provides maps and details about Santa Cruz. For broader island information, visit the Ministry of Tourism office (Binford and 12 de Febrero, tel. 5/252-6174, 9am-5pm Monday to Friday). The Galápagos National Park Office (tel. 5/252-6189, www.galapagospark.org) offers information and permits near the Charles Darwin Research Station.

Emergency services are located nearby, with the hospital at Baltra and Darwin (tel. 5/252-6103), and the police station behind the TAME airline office (tel. 5/252-6101).

Getting to and Around Santa Cruz Island

The primary airport serving Santa Cruz Island is Aeropuerto Seymour de Baltra (airport code: GPS). This airport is situated on Baltra Island, located just north of Santa Cruz. Upon arrival, getting to Puerto Ayora involves several steps. Start by taking a free airport bus right after the luggage claim area, which runs frequently and takes 15 minutes to reach the dock. From there, you'll take a ferry across the channel to Santa Cruz Island for $1; ferries depart every 15 minutes, with the crossing taking around 10 minutes. Once you arrive on Santa Cruz, a taxi to Puerto Ayora will take about 45 minutes and cost $25. Be mindful that taxis often exceed the 50 km/h (31 mph) speed limit, sometimes resulting in collisions with birds.

If you're looking for a more affordable and eco-friendly option, you can take the bus from the dock to Puerto Ayora for $2. The bus ride takes just over an hour, although the schedule is inconsistent, with buses departing based on flight arrivals and passenger numbers. Buses generally stop running by 10 a.m. For trips from Puerto Ayora to the dock, buses operate from 6:30 a.m. to 8:30 a.m. The bus station in Puerto Ayora is located at the terminal terrestre, which is either a long walk from downtown or a $1.50 taxi ride. If you miss the last bus, a taxi will be your only option.

For those needing to switch flights between the Galápagos and the mainland, airline offices for TAME (Darwin and 12 de Febrero, tel. 5/252-6527),

AeroGal (Rodríguez Lara and San Cristóbal, tel. 5/244-1950), and LAN (Darwin, www.latam.com) can be found in town.

Inter-Island Ferries

There are daily ferry services between Santa Cruz, San Cristóbal, and Isabela. Ferries to and from Floreana operate three to four times a week, though the schedule is less consistent, so it's advisable to check with local tourist agencies when planning your trip. All ferry routes cost $30 per person for a one-way trip and take approximately two hours. You can purchase tickets at kiosks near the dock or at any tour agency in town.

Speedboats leave Puerto Ayora for Isabela and San Cristóbal at 7 a.m. and 2 p.m., and for Floreana at 8 a.m. The return trip from Isabela departs at 6 a.m. and 3 p.m., from San Cristóbal at 7 a.m. and 2 p.m., and from Floreana at 3 p.m.

Inter-Island Flights

For those in a hurry or prone to seasickness, inter-island flights are a faster alternative. Emetebe (Los Colonos and Darwin, top floor, tel. 5/252-6177) and FlyGalápagos (tel. 5/301-6579, www.flyGalápagos.net) offer flights between San Cristóbal, Baltra, and Isabela on small eight-seat planes. Flights last about 30 minutes and operate several times a week. Prices start at $160 for a one-way ticket, with round-trip or two-flight combinations available from $240.

Getting Around Puerto Ayora

Within Puerto Ayora, white camioneta truck taxis are available for short trips around town, costing $1.50 per ride. However, since the town is quite small, many visitors find walking or renting a bike more convenient. If you wish to explore the highlands, taxi fares generally start at $40 for a half-day tour. Water taxis, which wait at the dock, offer transport to boats in the harbor for $0.80 per person during the day or $1 per person at night. These water taxis can also take you across to Angermeyer Point for visits to Playa de los Alemanes and Las Grietas.

SANTA CRUZ HIGHLANDS

Venturing into the highlands of Santa Cruz Island provides a refreshing contrast to the coastal environment, as you ascend to around 600 meters and discover misty forests and lush pastures. Guided tours, including visits to Los Gemelos, lava tunnels, and El Chato, can be booked as a half-day experience for approximately $40. Alternatively, independent travelers can access these attractions via bicycle or taxi.

Top Attraction

Tortoise Reserves

The highlight of the highlands is undoubtedly the tortoise reserves situated on private properties. Visitors often describe the experience as observing giant tortoises in a more natural setting compared to breeding enclosures. However, it's important to note that these reserves were once cattle ranches, with native escalesia forests replaced by grasslands. The wild giant tortoises roam freely between these private lands and adjacent national park areas, drawn by the availability of muddy ponds and fruit from introduced trees. Since the reserves are similar, most travelers choose to visit just one.

Approximately a 30-minute drive from Puerto Ayora lies El Chato Tortoise Reserve (no phone, open daily from 8 a.m. to 5 p.m., admission $5). Guests can explore the grounds independently, including the lava tunnels on-site. Be sure to visit the muddy pools where tortoises gather to cool off. A unique, albeit questionable, photo opportunity is available where visitors can don the heavy shell of a deceased tortoise. Entrance includes complimentary coffee and tea, and there is a restaurant serving decent almuerzos on the premises.

Another option is Rancho Primicias (no phone, open daily from 8 a.m. to 5 p.m., admission $5), a slightly less frequented private ranch offering views of giant tortoises and lava tunnels, located adjacent to El Chato.

Cerro Mesa, situated on the east side of the island at a higher elevation, is another viable choice (open daily, admission $5). While there are fewer giant tortoises and less developed walking paths compared to El Chato and Rancho Primicias, this location attracts fewer tourists. A lookout tower provides stunning 360-degree views of Santa Cruz Island, and a large collapsed crater is present, reminiscent of Los Gemelos. Good hiking shoes are recommended as the descent can be steep.

Los Gemelos

Just a few kilometers north of Santa Rosa are Los Gemelos, two 30-meter-deep craters formed by the collapse of lava caverns. The verdant interior of these craters is striking, and you may spot Galápagos hawks, barn owls, and vermilion flycatchers fluttering through the damp sceneries. The trail around these craters is short and typically takes no more than 15 minutes to explore.

Lava Tunnels

Lava tunnels are created by the outer crust of molten lava flows solidifying. These formations are often included in tours that visit the tortoise reserves and Los Gemelos. Popular reserves like El Chato or Rancho Primicias offer access to these tunnels as part of the admission fee. The largest lava tunnel at El Chato is well-lit and frequented by tour groups, while smaller tunnels may require a flashlight. Rancho Primicias features its own illuminated tunnel, which is longer, measuring about 600 meters (2,000 feet).

The most impressive lava tunnels can be found at Bellavista (admission $3.50), extending 2,200 meters (7,219 feet), though only a one-kilometer section is currently accessible to tourists. These tunnels offer a more authentic cave-exploring experience due to their longer lengths, fewer visitors, and natural rocky paths with minimal artificial lighting. Bellavista can be easily reached by bus from Puerto Ayora for $0.50.

Cerro Crocker and Puntudo

Hiking in this area is often overlooked by tour groups, presenting a chance to explore less-trafficked trails. The paths can be muddy, and much of the region has been affected by invasive plant species, leading to obstructed views due to fog. However, hikers may encounter lush endemic vegetation and, if fortunate, glimpses of the Galápagos petrel in the morning. On a clear day, Cerro Crocker– the highest point on the island– offers panoramic views.

To access the hiking trail, start at the trailhead located north of Bellavista, a small town north of Puerto Ayora. The journey to Media Luna, or "half moon," a volcanic formation blanketed in native miconia trees, is roughly two kilometers from the trailhead. Continuing north leads to a fork in the trail. The right path leads to Cerro Crocker, situated at an elevation of 860 meters (2,822 feet), about five kilometers (three miles) north of Media Luna. The left path leads to Puntudo, another peak that is less frequented. Hikers should be cautious; those attempting to hike directly between Cerro Crocker and Puntudo have reported getting lost due to the absence of a marked trail. A guide is advisable, but if you prefer to explore independently, bring friends and download an offline GPS map (maps.me is reliable). Fit hikers can complete this trek in three hours, but if you plan to backtrack and visit Puntudo, allow for an additional couple of hours.

To reach the trailhead, you can take a taxi from Puerto Ayora for about $10 per hour, which includes waiting time. Alternatively, a bus to Bellavista costs $0.50, followed by a three-kilometer uphill walk along a dirt road to the trailhead. This walk presents lovely scenery, passing through endemic escalesia trees and coffee farms, although it involves a significant elevation gain. Expect to budget an extra two hours for the walk up and down the dirt road. Another option is to arrange for a taxi drop-off directly at the trailhead for $18 and return downhill along the dirt road to Bellavista to catch the bus back to Puerto Ayora.

Galápagos Land Iguana

SANTA CRUZ ISLANDS

Santa Cruz Island, known for its rich biodiversity and stunning landscapes, offers a variety of unique experiences that draw visitors from around the globe. Whether you're seeking tranquil beaches or vibrant wildlife encounters, this island has something for everyone.

Top Attractions

Eastern Santa Cruz Island: El Garrapatero

El Garrapatero is situated 19 kilometers (12 miles) northeast of Puerto Ayora and stands out as one of the most picturesque beaches in the Galápagos archipelago. Nestled within a large, sheltered bay, it features calm turquoise waters that invite relaxation. Although it may not boast the length of Tortuga Bay, its more remote location means you'll often encounter fewer visitors. While snorkeling opportunities are limited, you can rent kayaks for $10 per person to explore the mangrove-lined shores and perhaps spot some elusive flamingos at the inland lagoon. Although walking on the beach is prohibited due to it being a tortoise nesting area, you can wade in the shallows or swim across to the opposite side of the bay, about 1.6 kilometers (1 mile) round-trip, if you are a strong swimmer—though the cloudy water may limit visibility. Taxis from Puerto Ayora to El Garrapatero cost around $40 for a round trip, including waiting time, or you can opt for a bike ride.

Bachas Beach

Bachas Beach, named after the remnants of U.S. military barges from World War II, features white sand often scattered with Sally Lightfoot crabs and serves as a nesting site for sea turtles. While the wrecks are usually buried, they can occasionally be glimpsed after high tides. This location is frequently included in cruise itineraries, especially those heading to Seymour Norte or Bartolomé, due to its proximity to the dock on the north side of Santa Cruz. However, independent visits to Bachas Beach are not permitted.

Black Turtle Cove

Located just west of the canal that connects Santa Cruz and Baltra, Black Turtle Cove is a shallow mangrove lagoon that extends inland. As there is no designated landing site, visitors can only tour the lagoon by panga (small boat). This area is teeming with birdlife, including herons and frigate birds, which nest among the red and white mangroves. Underwater, you might spot golden and spotted eagle rays, green sea turtles mating between September and February, and even white-tipped reef sharks resting in the shallows. Access to Black Turtle Cove is typically provided through cruise itineraries, often at the start or conclusion of trips due to its closeness to Baltra Airport.

Cerro Dragón (Dragon Hill)

On the northwest side of Santa Cruz, Cerro Dragón features a dry or wet landing depending on the tide. A lagoon often attracts flamingos, while a 2-kilometer (1.2-mile) trail weaves through the palo santo and opuntia cactus landscape, leading to panoramic views of volcanic tuff cones. Visitors here can encounter the land iguanas that lend the hill its name. Access to this site is only possible through organized cruises.

Surrounding Islands

- **Santa Fé Island**

Positioned midway between Santa Cruz and San Cristóbal, Santa Fé is approximately a two-hour boat ride from either island. Visitors can expect a wet landing on the northeast side, followed by trails through forests dominated by opuntia cacti, some reaching heights of 10 meters (33 feet). The terrain can be rocky, and hikers must navigate a steep ravine, making sturdy footwear essential. The island is home to the endemic yellowish Santa Fé iguana, and there's a chance of spotting Galápagos hawks. Popular for both cruises and day tours, trips to Santa Fé start at $160, while artisanal fishing tours, limited to snorkeling areas around the island, cost about $100.

- **Plaza Sur**

Located off the eastern coast of Santa Cruz, Plaza Sur is one of the smallest visitor sites in the Galápagos, covering just two square kilometers. The dry landing here is often greeted by lounging sea lions. A trail leads through a vibrant landscape to a section teeming with birdlife, including red-billed tropicbirds and frigate birds. The island's land iguanas are smaller and less colorful than those on Seymour Norte due to limited food resources and have adapted behaviors such as predation on birds. Visitors should be cautious around swimming or snorkeling due to potentially aggressive sea lion bulls. Day tours to Plaza Sur typically begin at $140.

- **Seymour Norte**

Seymour Norte, a small island off Santa Cruz's north coast, is renowned for its large colonies of blue-footed boobies and magnificent frigate birds. After a challenging dry landing on rocky terrain, you can trek along a 2.5-kilometer (1.6-mile) loop trail that takes over an hour to complete. The beaches here are often populated by marine iguanas, sea lions, and vibrant Sally Lightfoot crabs, while the surrounding waters offer excellent snorkeling opportunities to see sharks and tropical fish. Day tours to Seymour Norte start at $160 and are very popular among visitors.

- **Pinzón Islan**

East of Santa Cruz, Pinzón is recognized as one of the premier snorkeling locations accessible via day tours from Puerto Ayora. This island does not have a landing site, but its calm waters allow for sightings of diverse marine life, including sea lions, colorful fish, rays, sea turtles, and white-tipped sharks. Artisanal fishing day tours, which also provide opportunities to catch fish and enjoy a nearby beach, range from $100 to $140.

- **Daphne Major**

About 10 kilometers (6.2 miles) west of Seymour Norte, the Daphne Islands are generally excluded from most visitor itineraries due to restricted access. Daphne Major, the larger of the two islands, serves as a significant research site where scientists like Peter and Rosemary Grant studied finches, famously chronicled in the Pulitzer Prize-winning book The Beak of the Finch. Regular day trips for birdwatching, snorkeling, and fishing off Daphne's coast depart from Puerto Ayora, costing around $100 to $140. For the best experience, look for a tour that combines this destination with the exceptional snorkeling found at Pinzón.

SAN CRISTÓBAL

San Cristóbal, the easternmost and geologically oldest island in the Galápagos, is home to Puerto Baquerizo Moreno, the capital and administrative center of the archipelago. Unlike the bustling Puerto Ayora on Santa Cruz, Baquerizo Moreno maintains a quieter atmosphere, serving as a more modest tourism hub. Although it was once notorious as the site of a large penal colony in the late 19th century, today San Cristóbal offers a serene environment with excellent opportunities for boat trips into the national park, excursions to the highlands, and strolls along its beaches. However, for most visitors, a couple of days is sufficient to explore the island's highlights.

For a well-rounded experience, consider taking the 360 tour, which allows you to visit many of San Cristóbal's iconic sites, including the impressive León Dormido, all in a single day. On another day, embark on a trip to Española Island, known for its remarkable bird-watching opportunities and the presence of the waved albatross, a sight that was previously exclusive to cruise visitors. Dedicate your final day to visiting the Interpretation Center, climbing to the viewpoint for panoramic vistas, and snorkeling at Cerro Tijeretas. Don't miss the chance to observe the large sea lion colony at La Lobería in the afternoon. If time permits, consider additional snorkeling adventures with sea lions at Isla Lobos or a journey into the highlands.

San Cristóbal has made significant strides in renewable energy development. In response to an oil spill, wind turbines were installed in 2007, which have since provided 30 percent of the town's energy needs over the subsequent eight years. This initiative aligns with the government's ambitious Zero Fossil Fuel plan for the Galápagos Islands, aiming to eliminate fossil fuel reliance by 2020.

PUERTO BAQUERIZO MORENO

Puerto Baquerizo Moreno, the capital of the Galápagos Islands, offers a distinct experience compared to Puerto Ayora on Santa Cruz. This smaller, more affordable port town is not solely reliant on tourism; fishing and administrative activities also play significant roles in the local economy. Visitors will find a waterfront promenade where sea lions rest, particularly near the beach west of the center, which serves as a sleeping area for a large colony that congregates there at night. The strong smell of fish permeates the air, and it can be challenging to find spots along the boardwalk that are free from it. Nevertheless, Baquerizo Moreno is a favored destination with many attractions accessible either independently or through organized day tours. Among the highlights is Española Island, recognized as one of the premier sites in the archipelago, which has recently become accessible for day trips from the capital.

One of the popular destinations is **Playa Mann**, located a 10-minute walk northeast along Alsacio Northia. This beach tends to attract crowds on weekends, though the water quality is not particularly high. Across from the beach, a branch of the University of San Francisco de Quito frequently sees students visiting, adding to the local vibrancy. A small food stall offers basic meals, with prices starting around $8 for an almuerzo.

Moving east past Playa Mann, you'll find **Playa Punta Carola**, a beach sheltered by a rocky outcrop. It's a great spot for snorkeling, where sea turtles and sea lions can sometimes be spotted. It's best to visit during high tide due to the rocky landscape.

Continuing past Playa Punta Carola, a paved path leads to **Cerro Tijeretas**, a large hill with two viewpoints providing stunning vistas of the surrounding cove and beaches. The name "Tijeretas," which translates to "scissors" in

Spanish, refers to the distinctive tail shape of the frigate birds that inhabit the area. Early mornings are prime times to observe these magnificent birds soaring or resting in the trees. A protected cove below offers excellent swimming and snorkeling opportunities, particularly at high tide, with a wooden platform available for water entry. However, at low tide, navigating the rocky terrain can be challenging.

Beyond the lookout at Cerro Tijeretas, the path transforms into a rocky trail, with some sections requiring careful navigation over uneven lava rock. Although Playa Baquerizo is only 2 kilometers (1.2 miles) from this point, the trek often takes about an hour from Cerro Tijeretas, which itself is a 30-minute walk from town. This less-frequented beach provides a peaceful escape, perfect for swimming and snorkeling, though marine life is somewhat limited. It's advisable to wear sturdy hiking shoes and exercise caution after rainfall, as the combination of slippery mud and sharp lava rock can be hazardous.

Exploring these attractions can easily be accomplished in less than a day. Start with a morning visit to the **Interpretation Center** to gain insights into the Galápagos' history and environmental issues. From there, head to **Playa Punta Carola** for a refreshing swim and snorkeling session before ascending to the **Cerro Tijeretas viewpoint**. After enjoying the birdwatching, embark on the strenuous hike to **Playa Baquerizo**, where you can unwind, have lunch, and cool off in the waves. To break up the return hike, take a dip at the snorkeling site near Cerro Tijeretas.

Top Experiences in Puerto Baquerizo Moreno

Interpretation Center

To gain insight into the history and environmental challenges of the Galápagos Islands, head to the Interpretation Center, located a short walk from Playa Mann. Open daily from 8 AM to 5 PM, with no admission fee, this facility offers comprehensive exhibits on the islands' geology, development, and ecological issues. Many visitors find it even more informative than the smaller display at the Charles Darwin Research Station in Puerto Ayora.

La Lobería

At the opposite end of town from Playa Mann lies La Lobería, a rocky beach famous for its large sea lion colony. Reaching this location involves a 30-minute walk along an unmarked road near the airport, which offers little in terms of scenery aside from sparse cacti. To enhance your experience, consider biking or taking a taxi for about $4 to the trailhead, just a quarter mile from La Lobería. Here, you can walk among the sea lions, as dozens often lounge on the beach and rocks. While snorkeling is popular, it's best to visit during high tide to avoid shallow, rocky areas, and always be cautious of currents in the inlet. The trail from La Lobería spans approximately 1 kilometer (0.6 miles) and can be challenging due to loose lava rocks, so sturdy footwear is recommended.

Tours:

Highlands Tour

Experience the highlands on a half-day tour priced at around $40. This tour typically includes visits to La Galapaguera, Puerto Chino, El Junco, and sometimes Casa del Ceibo. For a budget-friendly option, consider hiring a taxi for about $10 per hour to reach these sites independently.

Bay Tour

For those interested in exploring the coastal waters, a half-day bay tour is available for $60, offered through kayak or stand-up paddleboard (SUP). Note that glass-bottom boats and dinghies are no longer permitted in the bay to protect wildlife.

Day Tours

Day trips to León Dormido cost approximately $100, while a trip to Isla Lobos is around $80, both of which include a nearby beach visit. Tours to Punta Pitt, priced at about $150, do not run daily and involve disembarking for a hike to the summit. The most extravagant option is a tour to see the waved albatross on Española Island, costing about $200.

Artisanal Fishing Tours

The 360 tour, priced at approximately $140, circumnavigates San Cristóbal and includes five sites in a single day. This tour kicks off with snorkeling in the tranquil lagoons of Bahía Rosa Blanca, followed by a scenic coastal route near Punta Pitt, where birdlife is plentiful (note that disembarking is not allowed here). A stop at the stunning white-sand beach of Bahía Sardinia provides relaxation, and the tour concludes with snorkeling at León Dormido, also featuring a fishing stop where you might enjoy freshly prepared ceviche. Total navigation time is about four hours, making it unsuitable for those prone to seasickness.

Tour Operators and Agencies

Several agencies in Puerto Baquerizo Moreno offer a variety of tours and rentals:

Lava Wave Surf (tel. 5/252-1815, info@lavawavesurf.com) provides surfboard rentals, classes, yoga sessions, and guided biking tours. They can also arrange other tours on the island.

León Dormido Tours (Villamil at Darwin, tel. 99/445-1667, leondormidogalapagos.com.ec) is a well-regarded agency that offers bike rentals, diving excursions, ferry tickets, and day tours.

SUP Galápagos (Malecón at Melville, tel. 93/967-8592, reservas@Galápagos.tours) is the sole provider of stand-up paddleboarding tours in the area.

For diving excursions, it's best to contact dive operators directly:

Dive and Surf Club (Melville, tel. 8/087-7122 or 8/634-7256, divesurfclub.com) offers daily dive tours, discovery dives, PADI courses, and night dives.

Scuba Eden (Teodoro Wolf and Darwin, tel. 5/252-0666, scubaedengalapagos.com) runs daily snorkeling and dive trips to Kicker Rock.

Galápagos Blue Evolution (Melville at Hernández, tel. 5/301-0264, Galápagosblueevolution.com.ec) provides a complete range of dive certifications, from open water to dive master.

Outdoor Activities

Surfing

San Cristóbal is known for its vibrant surfing culture. Board rentals are available for $20 per day. Head east past the military base along Armada Nacional to discover prime surfing spots such as El Cañon and Tongo, which are best suited for experienced surfers due to rocky conditions and lack of beach access. Identification is required to pass through the military base. Other popular surfing locations include Punta Carola at the west end of town and Manglecito, which is only reachable by boat.

Biking

Many local agencies offer mountain bike rentals for $20 per day or $10 for a half day. Cycling to the highlands is an enjoyable option, as a designated bike lane extends partway toward the highlands. However, be prepared for a strenuous day if you plan to go all the way to Puerto Chino and back.

Kayaking

Guided kayaking tours cost around $60 and depart from the port to explore the bay, coastline, or snorkeling spots at Tijeretas. Longer kayaking excursions to Playa Ochoa are rare, and independent kayaking is not allowed due to safety concerns.

Diving

San Cristóbal offers excellent diving opportunities, although fewer operators are based here. A hyperbaric chamber is located at the Port Capitania. Most dive trips range from $140 to $160, while excursions to Punta Pitt or Española can cost between $200 and $250. For those without certification, open water dive courses are available, as well as advanced level, rescue diver, and dive master training.

Recommended dive sites include Tijeretas and the Caragua wreck, suitable for divers needing a skills refresher, with Tijeretas being a shallow area rich in tropical fish. The Caragua wreck, the remains of a boat associated with the infamous Manuel J. Cobos, now forms an artificial reef teeming with fish.

Kicker Rock is the most renowned dive site, where divers frequently encounter hammerhead sharks, sea lions, eagle rays, and stingrays, accommodating all skill levels.

Diving at Punta Pitt includes a short hike to observe red-footed boobies and two immersion dives at Cerro Pitt and Bajo Pitt, featuring diverse marine life. However, expect a lengthy boat ride and a higher price tag.

Additionally, a dive trip to Española encompasses visits to Punta Suárez, where the waved albatross resides, along with two dives in nearby waters.

For advanced divers, locations such as Islote 5 Fingers, Roca Este, and Roca Ballena offer encounters with various shark species and vibrant marine life. The Hitler Caves, three large underwater caves, provide calm waters for exploration, named after a local fisherman with no connection to historical figures.

Dining Options in Puerto Baquerizo Moreno

While Puerto Baquerizo Moreno may not boast the same culinary variety as Puerto Ayora, it offers several local eateries that cater to different tastes. Family-run establishments serve a mix of Ecuadorian fare and fast food, while a few upscale seafood restaurants diversify their menus with pizza and pasta, though options for international cuisine are limited.

Snack Shops

For those craving a quick bite, **Panadería Cuencan Taste** located at Northia, offers a variety of baked goods. Open Monday through Saturday from 2 PM to 9 PM, this popular bakery is known for its rolls, which range in price from $0.25 to $0.50, alongside treats such as empanadas and chocolate rolls.

Ecuadorian Cuisine and Seafood

Numerous informal dining spots provide breakfast, burgers, sandwiches, and snacks. On the malecón, **Patagonia** (tel. 5/252-0017) serves breakfast, lunch, and dinner daily from $5 to $10, making it one of the few venues offering early breakfast options before day tours. Similarly, **Tongo Reef Bar** (tel. 5/252-1852), open daily, offers similar fare within the same price range. Their breakfast menu includes both American and continental options, alongside local specialties like bolon-fried plantain balls.

For a livelier café atmosphere, **Casa Blanca Café** at the intersection of Malecón and Melville provides breakfast, lunch, and dinner for $5 to $12 daily. While sandwiches are just average, it's a favored spot for traditional snacks such as tamales and humitas, especially at sunset.

For a budget-friendly meal, **Lucky's (Villamil and Hernández)** is a local favorite. Open Monday through Friday from 8 AM to 9 PM and Saturday to Sunday from 8 AM to 2 PM, this small eatery offers a two-course lunch and dinner for $4, as well as simple breakfast options.

Cevicheria Delicias del Mar (Northia and Melville), open daily from 8:30 AM to 3 PM, is where locals flock for ceviche, available for $10 to $12. Diners can enjoy various ceviche options, including basic fish or mixed seafood varieties, all served with fried banana chips and popcorn.

Rosita (Villamil and Hernández, tel. 5/252-1581) attracts both tourists and locals with its casual atmosphere. Open daily from noon to 3 PM and 5 PM to 10 PM, the menu includes fish, shellfish, and meat dishes priced from $15 to $20. The restaurant also offers a set meal for $6, ensuring good value.

Descanso Marinero (Northia and Melville) features a fun tropical atmosphere, with large portions of delicious food priced between $15 and $20. Open daily from 8 AM to 9 PM, this restaurant serves a variety of rice, chicken, shrimp, and fish dishes, with a specialty in sizzling a la plancha options.

International Cuisine

For an exceptional burger, head to **Cri's Burger Factory** (Teodoro Wolf and Hernández, tel. 99/423-6770). This local hotspot, open daily from 5 PM to 10 PM and offering burgers priced from $7 to $12, is known for its substantial patties and unique toppings. Other menu items include pizza, hot dogs, and salads.

Fresco's is a laid-back restaurant near Playa Mann, serving breakfast for $4 and almuerzos for $8 from 7:30 AM to 6 PM daily. Their fresh dishes, like avocado and egg toast, and espresso drinks stand out for their quality, especially since everything is cooked to order. While they close at 6 PM, snacks are available after 3 PM.

Giuseppe's (Darwin at Manuel Cobos, tel. 99/763-8540) specializes in Italian cuisine, including pizza, pasta, and seafood dishes, with prices ranging from $10 to $20.

Nativo (Malecón) offers an informal dining experience from 10 AM to 10 PM daily for $10 to $20. Their menu includes salads, pizzas, and wings, all made with local ingredients, ensuring a fresh dining experience.

Calypso (Darwin and Cobos, tel. 5/252-0154) is popular with tourists, known for its breezy outdoor tables and deep-dish pizza priced between $10 and $15, alongside other dishes like seafood and burgers.

The top dining establishment in Puerto Baquerizo Moreno is **Muyu** (Malecón inside Golden Bay Hotel, tel. 05/252-0069), offering a farm-and-sea-to-table dining experience. Open daily for breakfast from 7 AM to 10 AM, lunch from noon to 3 PM, and dinner from 5 PM to 10 PM, prices for entrées range from $20 to $35, with a tasting menu available for $65. While the menu bar offers meal-size bites for $7, this restaurant prides itself on sourcing ingredients from the Galápagos for superior quality.

Markets

For those looking to prepare their own meals, the town features several small convenience stores with limited fruit, vegetable, and meat selections. The main supermarket, located at Quito and Flores, also has a modest selection of fresh produce.

The Municipal Market (12 de Febrero and Flores), open from 6 AM to 6 PM Monday through Friday, 4 AM to 2 PM Saturday, and 6 AM to noon Sunday, offers a wider selection of fruits and vegetables. However, much of the food is imported during the week, leading to higher prices. On Saturdays, local farms bring organic produce to sell.

Seafood lovers can find fresh catches, including lobster, at the **Muelle de Pescadores** (fishing dock), typically available from 7 AM until sold out. Lobster season runs from September 8 to January 8, while langostino is available for the remainder of the year.

Accommodations

Puerto Baquerizo Moreno has a range of accommodations, particularly in the budget category, while options for midrange and high-end hotels are less common. This scarcity is beneficial as it keeps the town quieter compared to Santa Cruz, where tour groups prefer to stay.

Budget Accommodations Under $50

For budget travelers, **Casa de Laura** (Callejón 2 and Armada, tel. 5/252-0173, www.hostalcasadelaura.com) offers an excellent choice at $20 per person. Located at the end of a quiet cul-de-sac, this family-run hostal features bright, air-conditioned rooms with views of a lush tropical garden.

Another family-operated option is **Casa de Huéspedes Milena** (Serrano at Northia, tel. 99/013-6604, milepibu11@hotmail.com), priced at $25 per person, which offers well-maintained rooms closer to the coast.

Hostal León Dormido (Jose de Villamil and Malecón, tel. 5/252-0169) provides basic but comfortable guest rooms for $25 per single and $50 per double. With a small coffee shop on-site, guests can enjoy some amenities.

Casa Mabell (Melville and Northia, tel. 98/125-8617) offers both single rooms for $30 and doubles for $40, along with a shared kitchen for those who prefer to cook.

Midrange Accommodations $50-$100

Hostal Andry (12 de Febrero at Ignacio Hernández, tel. 5/252-1652, hostal_andry@outlook.es) offers good value with simple rooms starting at $30. Located centrally, it includes a tourist agency for convenience.

Hostal Galápagos (Playa de Oro, tel. 05/301-0947, www.hostalgalapagos.com) has some of the most affordable beach-view accommodations, with prices between $50 and $60.

Located just inland, **Hostal Casa de Nelly** (Tijeretas and Manuel Agama, tel. 5/252-0112, saltosnelly@hotmail.com) offers pleasant rooms starting at $50, featuring rustic decor and a shared kitchen.

La Zayapa (Darwin at Melville, tel. 99/643-9541, www.lazayapahotel.com) has modern rooms priced from $60 to $90. While interior rooms lack views, those facing the bay provide spectacular sights.

Casa Blanca (Malecón and Melville, tel. 5/252-0392, www.casablancagalapagos.com) is notable for its stunning architecture and rooms with beautiful views, priced from $70 to $120.

Luxury Accommodations Over $200

For a premium experience, **Hotel Katarma** (Northia and Esmeraldas, tel. 5/252-0300) features only 13 rooms set around a lovely courtyard, with rates of $170 for singles and $200 for doubles.

Galápagos Sunset Hotel (Charles Darwin at Melville, tel. 5/252-0529, http://Galápagossunset.com.ec) is an upscale boutique hotel, with daily rates of $138 for doubles and $220 for ocean-view suites, providing panoramic vistas.

Casa Opuntia (Darwin, tel. 2/604-6800 in Quito, www.opuntiaGalápagostours.com) is renowned for its elegant accommodations, offering rooms between $120 and $220. The property includes a beautiful restaurant with open-air seating.

Puerto Baquerizo Moreno offers a range of accommodations, particularly suited for budget travelers. While the options for mid-range and luxury hotels are limited, this creates a quieter environment, as many tour groups prefer the more populated Santa Cruz.

Budget-Friendly Stays Under $50

Travelers seeking affordable lodging will find many family-run hostels in the area. These often converted residences may be located a bit farther from the central area, resulting in limited accessibility, and tend to have staff that primarily speak Spanish, as well as inconsistent Wi-Fi. Most budget hostels do not include breakfast unless specified, and while many rooms come with private bathrooms, this may vary.

One notable option is **Casa de Laura** (Callejón 2 and Armada, tel. 5/252-0173, www.hostalcasadelaura.com, $20 per person). Nestled at the end of a quiet street, this hostel provides a peaceful retreat with its air-conditioned rooms overlooking a beautiful tropical garden. Guests can unwind in hammocks and enjoy the welcoming lounge.

Another option is **Casa de Huéspedes Milena** (Serrano at Northia, tel. 99/013-6604, milepibu11@hotmail.com, $25 per person), which features spacious and well-kept guest rooms situated slightly inland, providing easy access to local attractions.

Hostal León Dormido (Jose de Villamil and Malecón, tel. 5/252-0169, $25 for a single room, $50 for a double) is conveniently located with modest accommodations that include air-conditioning and a cozy lounge area.

For those who prefer to cook, **Casa Mabell** (Melville and Northia, tel. 98/125-8617, $30 for a single, $40 for a double) is one of the few hostels offering shared kitchen facilities. Rooms are cozy, modern, and equipped with air-conditioning and a TV.

High-End Experiences

For those seeking an intimate stay, the **boutique Casa Iguana Mar y Sol** (Alsacio Northia, tel. 5/252-1788, http://casaiguanamarysol.com, $135-285 for a double) features five spacious suites, each with large beds, sitting areas, and stunning bay views. The property, modern yet infused with tropical touches, was established in 2009.

The luxurious Golden Bay Hotel & Spa (Playa del Oro, tel. 5/252-0069, www.goldenbay.com.ec, $305-410 for a double, $525 for a suite) stands out as the most lavish option in San Cristóbal. Guests enjoy plush beds, rainfall showers, an on-site spa, and sweeping views through floor-to-ceiling windows. Additional amenities include a pool, a rooftop terrace with a hot tub, and the renowned Muyu restaurant offering farm- and sea-to-table dining. For an extra touch of luxury, book a suite equipped with a soaking tub.

Information and Services in Puerto Baquerizo Moreno

For travelers seeking information, the CAPTURGAL tourist information office (Hernández, tel. 5/252-1124, 8 am-noon and 2 pm-5 pm Mon.-Fri.) and the municipal tourist office (Darwin and 12 de Febrero, tel. 5/252-0119 or 5/252-0358, 8 am-noon and 2 pm-5 pm Mon.-Fri.) offer maps and useful information.

While many cafés and hotels provide Wi-Fi, expect slow connection speeds.

Additional services in the town include a post office located at the western end of Darwin, beyond the municipal building; the police station (Darwin and Española, tel. 5/252-0101); and the Oscar Jandl Hospital (Northia and Quito, tel. 5/252-0118), which provides basic medical care and operates a 24-hour emergency room.

Transportation Options for San Cristóbal

Accessing San Cristóbal Airport

San Cristóbal Airport (SCY) is situated at the western end of Avenida Alsacio Northia, just past the local radio station. To reach Puerto Baquerizo Moreno from the airport, you can opt for a taxi, which costs approximately $2, or enjoy a leisurely 20-minute walk.

Interisland Ferry Services

Getting around the Galápagos Islands is straightforward, thanks to the daily interisland ferry services. These small launches facilitate travel between Santa Cruz, San Cristóbal, and Isabela, with a one-way fare of $30 per person and a travel time of about two hours. Ferries depart from Puerto Ayora on Santa Cruz at 7 am and 2 pm for San Cristóbal. Conversely, ferries from San Cristóbal back to Puerto Ayora also leave at 7 am and 2 pm.

If you aim to travel from San Cristóbal to Isabela in one day, you'll need to take two ferries, which can be uncomfortable. The first leg involves taking the 7 am ferry from San Cristóbal to Puerto Ayora, followed by the afternoon ferry at 2 pm from Puerto Ayora to Isabela. For the return trip, catch the 6 am ferry from Isabela to Puerto Ayora, and then take the 2 pm ferry from Puerto Ayora back to San Cristóbal. Unfortunately, same-day travel from San Cristóbal to Floreana is not feasible due to the ferry schedule.

Interisland Flights

For those preferring air travel, small eight-seat planes operate half-hour flights connecting San Cristóbal with Baltra and Isabela several times a week. One-way fares start at $156, while round-trip tickets or any two flights cost $240. You can book these interisland flights through Emetebe (tel./fax 5/252-0615, www.emetebe.com.ec) or FlyGalápagos (tel. 5/301-6579, www.flyGalápagos.net).

Local Transportation in Puerto Baquerizo Moreno

Within Baquerizo Moreno, taxis are a convenient and budget-friendly option, with fares only $1 for short trips. If you wish to explore the highlands, you can hire a taxi for around $10 per hour. Additionally, buses depart from the malecón several times a day to El Progreso in the highlands, or you can take a taxi for approximately $3.

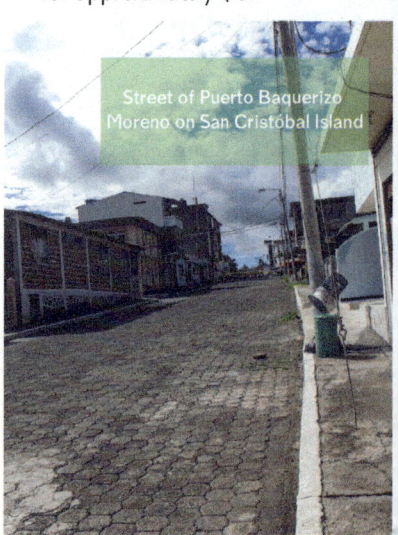

Street of Puerto Baquerizo Moreno on San Cristóbal Island

OFF THE COAST

Exploring Isla Lobos

Isla Lobos, a small rocky island located just 30 minutes north of Baquerizo Moreno by boat, is a prime spot for snorkeling. While walking on the island is prohibited to preserve its wildlife, visitors can dive right into the water to experience excellent snorkeling alongside playful sea lions in the channel that separates the islet from the mainland. Birdwatchers can also spot nesting boobies and frigate birds. Day trips to Isla Lobos cost around $80 and often include a visit to a nearby beach, providing opportunities for sunbathing and swimming.

Discovering Bahía Rosa Blanca

Bahía Rosa Blanca offers a serene environment perfect for snorkeling enthusiasts. This tranquil bay is known for its clear, protected waters that shift to vibrant shades of turquoise under sunlight. Here, snorkelers can encounter a diverse array of marine life, including colorful fish, white-tipped reef sharks, and sea turtles seeking refuge in these inviting waters. Access to Bahía Rosa Blanca is exclusively available through the 360 tour, which departs from Puerto Baquerizo Moreno and provides a scenic circumnavigation of the island.

Kicker Rock (León Dormido) Adventures

Kicker Rock, or León Dormido, is one of the most iconic landmarks in the Galápagos. Shaped like a lion or a foot, this volcanic tuff cone is renowned for its exceptional snorkeling and diving experiences. The structure features steep walls, with a narrow channel that attracts marine life. Snorkelers can frequently spot white-tipped reef sharks in the area, while divers may encounter impressive schools of hammerheads, along with sea turtles and various rays. Due to preservation efforts, boats are prohibited from entering the channel and must wait at both ends while you snorkel or dive. Day trips for snorkeling in this area are priced at $100 and typically include a stop at one of three beautiful beaches—Cerro Brujo, Puerto Grande, or Manglecito—offering opportunities for relaxed swimming and sunbathing. Among these, Cerro Brujo is often highlighted as the most stunning, boasting a long stretch of white sand flanked by rugged cliffs, with occasional kayaking excursions.

Venturing to Punta Pitt

Punta Pitt, located at the northeastern tip of San Cristóbal, is the most remote site from the port. Visiting Punta Pitt involves a wet landing followed by a strenuous two-hour round-trip hike uphill, where visitors navigate through thorny scrub and past distinctive tuff cones. The effort is rewarded with breathtaking panoramic views and the chance to observe the only colony of red-footed boobies in the Galápagos outside of Genovesa, as well as the opportunity to see all three species of boobies coexisting. This area is also home to frigate birds, storm petrels, and swallow-tailed gulls. Punta Pitt is a common stop on cruise ship itineraries, and day tours from Baquerizo Moreno are available, though only a few agencies offer these trips, charging a premium price of $150 to $200. Additionally, 360 tours may pass by Punta Pitt without disembarking, allowing for distant birdwatching before continuing on their journey.

Sunset at Puerto Baquerizo Moreno

SAN CRISTÓBAL HIGHLANDS

The San Cristóbal Highlands is accessible through guided tours priced at approximately $40 per person, or you can opt to share a taxi, which starts at around $10 per hour. For those who prefer cycling, bike rentals are available in town for about $20 a day; however, be aware that the ride to the farthest points is challenging, with a steep incline over 25 kilometers one way. A popular strategy is to hire a taxi to drop you off at higher altitudes, such as Laguna El Junco, allowing you to bike downhill to La Galapaguera and Puerto Chino before making your way back uphill.

Attractions

Casa del Ceibo

To reach Casa del Ceibo, follow Avenida 12 de Febrero as it climbs north out of Baquerizo Moreno towards El Progreso, a quiet farming community that was once a penal colony. Although the village itself has little to offer, Casa del Ceibo provides a unique attraction located near the main street (phone: 5/252-0248; website: www.lacasadelceibo.com). This distinctive tree house nestled in a massive kapok tree—reportedly the world's widest at eight meters—allows guests to rappel up, lounge in hammocks, and savor local coffee. Visitors can enjoy a brief stay in this quirky accommodation, which accommodates two people overnight for $25 per person, with visiting hours from 9 a.m. to 12:30 p.m. and 1:30 p.m. to 5:30 p.m. daily, charging an entrance fee of $1.50.

Laguna El Junco

From El Progreso, the road continues north to Soledad and east towards Cerro Verde and Los Arroyos. About 10 kilometers east of Progreso, a steep dirt track leads to Laguna El Junco, one of the few freshwater lakes in the Galápagos situated 700 meters (2,300 feet) above sea level within a collapsed caldera. This lake is replenished by rainwater and is home to various wading birds, frigate birds, Chatham mockingbirds, and seven species of Darwin's finches. It's also a great spot for observing the highland tree ferns. A scenic trail encircles the lake, offering panoramic views that can be enjoyed on a leisurely 45-minute walk. Be cautious during the rainy season (January to April), as the area can become muddy.

Puerto Chino

Continuing from Cerro Verde, you will arrive at Puerto Chino, a secluded beach on the south coast popular among local surfers. While swimming and snorkeling are discouraged due to strong currents, a viewpoint on the right side of the beach allows for the observation of blue-footed boobies. Camping is permitted here with prior approval from the national park office located in the port, but ensure you bring your own camping gear. For budget travelers, a bus service operates on Sundays, departing from the mercado in Puerto Baquerizo Moreno to Puerto Chino for $2. The buses leave the market at 8 a.m. and 9 a.m., with return trips from the beach at 4 p.m.

La Galapaguera

Located a few kilometers inland from Puerto Chino, La Galapaguera is a giant tortoise reserve open daily from 6 a.m. to 6 p.m. and free of charge. This 12-hectare reserve provides a sanctuary for San Cristóbal tortoises, allowing them to breed in a natural setting. Baby tortoises are safeguarded from invasive species until they reach five years of age and are housed in elevated enclosures. Mature tortoises roam freely across the stone pathways, offering visitors a chance to observe these remarkable creatures up close.

Castillo San Cristóbal

QUICK NOTE

"I hope this chapter proved informative. Your feedback on the book thus far is highly valued and will be used to enhance future editions. Please take a moment to share your thoughts by dropping a review on Amazon. Thank you, and enjoy the rest of the book."

ISABELA

Isabela Island stands out as the largest in the Galápagos archipelago, covering nearly 4,600 square kilometers (1,776 square miles) and constituting half of the total land area of the islands. Stretching 100 kilometers (62 miles) in length, it is four times larger than Santa Cruz, the second-largest island. Isabela is one of the youngest islands in the group, characterized by its striking terrain shaped by six intermittently active volcanoes. These volcanoes, from north to south, include Wolf (1,646 meters/5,400 feet), Ecuador (610 meters/2,000 feet), Darwin (1,280 meters/4,200 feet), Alcedo (1,097 meters/3,600 feet), Sierra Negra (1,490 meters/4,888 feet), and Cerro Azul (1,250 meters/4,100 feet).

Isabela is home to one of the largest populations of giant tortoises in the Galápagos, which thrive on the lush vegetation found in the highlands. There are five distinct subspecies of tortoises, each associated with a specific volcano, except for the smaller Volcán Ecuador. Notably, the slopes of Volcán Alcedo host over 35 percent of the tortoise population across the archipelago.

The island's west coast benefits from the nutrient-rich waters of the Humboldt and Cromwell Currents, contributing to a vibrant marine ecosystem. This area is teeming with wildlife, including large numbers of whales, dolphins, and flightless cormorants, which have adapted to diving for fish without the use of wings. Isabela also boasts the highest concentration of Galápagos penguins.

Puerto Villamil is Isabela's primary port, home to around 2,000 residents. While it is gradually evolving into a tourism hub, it remains on a much smaller scale compared to Puerto Ayora. Numerous visitor attractions are conveniently located near the port, alongside opportunities for excursions to the volcanoes inland. However, many of the most remarkable coastal sites are situated on Isabela's west side, which are primarily accessible via cruises. Due to the distance, most cruises focus on the central and southern islands, with fewer than 25 percent venturing to Isabela. Those that do are rewarded with breathtaking destinations.

Attractions and Activities
Visitors staying in Puerto Villamil can explore several noteworthy sites, including **the Tortoise Breeding Center**, the largest of its kind in the archipelago. Nearby, the islets of Las Tintoreras offer excellent snorkeling opportunities with reef sharks, while the stunning **archways of Los Túneles** provide additional chances for underwater exploration. A highlight of Isabela is the hike to Sierra Negra, which features the second-largest active crater in the world.

Marine sites accessible exclusively by cruise boats include panga (dinghy) rides through the **mangroves of Punta Moreno**, where penguins can be observed, and trips to **Elizabeth Bay**, home to the flightless cormorants. **Urbina Bay** is noteworthy for its fascinating raised coral reef, while **Tagus Cove** attracts attention for its historical graffiti left by pirates and a hike to the deep-blue saline Darwin Lake.

Galápagos penguin on Isabela Island

PUERTO VILLAMIL

Nestled on the southeastern tip of Isabela, Puerto Villamil is a quaint port with a population of approximately 2,000 residents. The community thrives on fishing and a budding tourism sector, while also engaging in various local ventures such as sulfur mining at the nearby Sierra Negra volcano, lime production, and coffee cultivation. This charming town presents a more relaxed atmosphere compared to the larger ports in the Galápagos. Visitors will find a limited selection of hotels and restaurants, along with pristine beaches, a serene lagoon, and opportunities for highland hikes, making Puerto Villamil an ideal spot to unwind for a few days. Note that there is no ATM on the island, and cash is essential as credit cards are rarely accepted.

Attractions

Playa Grande

The main beach of Puerto Villamil, Playa Grande, features a stunning three-kilometer stretch of white sand perfect for leisurely strolls, swimming, and sunset watching. Starting from the town, the beach is marked by a rustic wooden lookout and becomes increasingly pristine as you head west. Keep an eye out for blue-footed boobies, often spotted diving in synchronized feeding frenzies.

Concha de Perla

For snorkeling enthusiasts, Concha de Perla offers a complimentary and accessible spot for underwater exploration. Bring your own snorkeling gear or rent equipment in town, then take a leisurely 15-minute walk toward the dock. No guide or taxi is required. This sheltered cove features calm waters teeming with fish, sea lions, and rays, with a raised wooden path winding through mangroves leading to the dock.

Tours and Excursions

Highlands Tours

A highlight of any visit to Isabela is the hike to Sierra Negra Volcano and Volcán Chico, available for around $40. Many tours include a downhill biking option back to town. For those seeking a more unique experience, private tours to the sulfur mines can be arranged at a cost of $100 per person, with a minimum of four participants.

Bay Tours

The Tintoreras Bay half-day tour, priced at $40, is an excellent way to explore snorkeling opportunities around the islet, take a short hike through lava fields, and observe a channel where whitetipped reef sharks rest. Alternative options include kayaking and stand-up paddleboard (SUP) tours of the bay, priced at $50 each, but these do not include disembarkation.

Artisanal Fishing Tours

The artisanal fishing tour to Los Túneles is highly regarded at $110 and is considered one of the best excursions from Puerto Villamil. Although less popular, the tour to Isla Tortuga also costs $110 and operates on a less frequent schedule, featuring a chance to catch fish for lunch.

Tour Operators and Agencies

GalaTourEx (Gil, tel. 5/252-9324, galatourex2017@hotmail.com) can assist with organizing an overnight stay at Campo Duro EcoLodge for camping at $70, in addition to offering tours for $48 that include a hike to Sierra Negra along with breakfast and a buffet lunch at Campo Duro. Most other tour operators provide box lunches.

Rosadelco Tour (Conocarpus at Pinzón, tel. 5/252-9237 or 99/4949693,

http://rosedelco.com.ec) is a trusted local operator offering tours to Los Túneles, Sierra Negra Volcano, Tintoreras, and snorkeling at Isla Tortuga.

Galápagos Bike & Surf (Escalesias at Tero Real, tel. 99/488-5473 or 5/252-9509,

www.Galápagosbikeandsurf.com) provides surfing classes at $45, surfboard rentals for $25 per full day or $15 for half a day, and bike rentals for $20 per day. They are the only company in town that offers SUP tours to Tintoreras, priced at $50, which include snorkeling. They also conduct Sierra Negra tours with downhill biking a couple of times a week.

Recreation and Activities

Biking

Puerto Villamil offers excellent biking opportunities, allowing visitors to explore the far end of Playa Grande, the Los Humedales, and the Wall of Tears independently. More adventurous cyclists can ascend into the lush highland areas where local farms are located, though this involves a steep climb. A less challenging option is to rent a mountain bike and take a taxi to El Cura for $25, then bike downhill.

When renting a bike (approximately $15 per day), ask the travel agency to make reservations at one of the highland restaurants for lunch. Popular spots include Campo Duro, which features a campground and a giant tortoise reserve, Flor de Recuerdo, a family-run farm known for its chicken cooked on lava rocks, and Hauser's, an upscale restaurant with a refined dining experience. After lunch, consider visiting the volcanic caves at Cuevas de Sucre.

Diving

For diving enthusiasts, Isla Tortuga presents an intermediate dive site located just 30 minutes from the port, where divers can encounter giant manta rays and hammerhead sharks in relatively calm waters. While advanced dive sites such as Cuatro Hermanos and La Viuda are available, finding day tours can be challenging due to the popularity of Isla Tortuga and a limited number of dive operators on the island.

Isla Bella Tour (Antonio Gil and Escalesias, tel. 5/252-9151, harrymoscoso@yahoo.com) is the sole dive operator on Isabela, offering trips to Isla Tortuga most days for $150. Unlike Puerto Ayora, Isabela lacks a hyperbaric chamber.

Another option is Natural Selection Tours (Gil at Escalesias, tel. 96/837-6151, http://Galápagosnaturalselection.com), which conducts discovery dives near Tintoreras but does not venture to Isla Tortuga. They also offer PADI open water dive certification.

Nightlife in Puerto Villamil

The nightlife in Puerto Villamil is relaxed, featuring a few bars and a couple of local dance clubs. The most frequented spot is **Caleta Iguana Bar**, located at the Caleta Iguana hostal. It operates from 7 PM to midnight, Monday to Saturday. This beachfront venue offers a laid-back atmosphere perfect for watching the sunset, especially during its happy hour from 5 PM to 7 PM. Guests can enjoy the challenge of walking on a slackline or unwind in hammocks and by a beach bonfire.

For a quieter drink, head next door to **Bar Beto**, also open from 7 PM to midnight, Monday to Saturday. This beach bar at the western edge of town provides a great sea view, though the cocktails tend to be on the pricier side.

Dining Options in Puerto Villamil

Restaurant choices in Puerto Villamil are limited, with most establishments located along the main road, Antonio Gil, and the malecón. Visitors should note that dining prices are generally higher here than in Puerto Ayora or Puerto Baquerizo Moreno due to the costs associated with food importation.

For affordable eats, **the Mercado Municipal** (16 de Marzo) operates daily from 7 AM to 6 PM, closing for lunch from noon to 2 PM. Here, you can find basic breakfast and lunch options, such as fried empanadas priced at $1. However, dinner is not served at the market.

The south side of the main square features a selection of casual restaurants that cater mainly to tourists. While the food is decent, expect simple offerings of rice, beans, small portions of protein, and limited vegetables, with meals costing around $6 for breakfast and $8 for lunch or dinner.

El Cafetal, located at Fragatas and Gil, welcomes guests from 9 AM to 1 PM and 3 PM to 10 PM daily. Reservations are recommended due to its popularity. The menu, priced between $15 and $25, includes pasta, sandwiches, and seafood, all served in a pleasant atmosphere that enhances the dining experience.

S Coco Surf, situated at Gil and 16 de Marzo, opens from noon to 2 PM and 6 PM to 9 PM, Monday to Saturday, and from 6 PM to 9 PM on Sunday. The focus here is on fresh island ingredients, with dishes like patacón pisao, topped with crab or beef, and a delicious seafood fajita, priced between $12 and $25. The casual setting may look unassuming, but the quality of food is well-known among locals.

For those seeking a lively atmosphere, **La Casa del Asado** at Av. Mercado Municipal and Cormoran operates daily from 6:30 PM to 10 PM. Dishes range from $7 to $12, with grill platters for two at $20, popular among the local crowd. The mixed seafood grill is particularly recommended.

If you're in the mood for various meats, **Isabela Grill** at 16 de Marzo and Los Jelies is open from 10 AM to 2 PM and 5 PM to 10 PM daily, offering an indoor escape from mosquitoes. Their menu features everything from T-bone to filet mignon, along with chicken and seafood dishes, priced between $15 and $25.

For those craving international flavors, **Sun & Coffee** at Gil and Petreles welcomes guests from 7 AM to noon and 5 PM to 10 PM daily, offering sandwiches and crepes priced at $6 to $14, and entrées from $15 to $20. The café-deli is known for its espresso drinks and seafood specialties.

Booby Trap, located at Gil, operates from 11 AM to 3 PM and 5 PM to 8:30 PM, Tuesday to Sunday. Dishes range from $8 to $20, with lobster priced at $30. The menu features fresh ingredients and generous portions, with a particularly recommended tuna-avocado-octopus tartare.

Casa Marita Restaurant at Gil, operating from 7 AM to 8:30 PM daily, offers a delightful dining experience priced between $15 and $25. Located on the third floor of Casa Marita Hotel, it features Peruvian ceviche and seafood dishes inspired by the owners' heritage.

Iguana Crossing, the town's only gourmet restaurant, is located at Gil and opens from 7 AM to 9 PM daily, serving local and international cuisine priced at $20 to $25. The menu includes grilled seafood and creative dishes like passionfruit chicken and coconut lobster.

Shopping for Ingredients in Puerto Villamil

If you're staying in a hostel equipped with a kitchen, self-catering is feasible, although the variety of ingredients in Puerto Villamil is limited compared to Puerto Ayora. Fresh produce can be sourced from the municipal market located at 16 de Marzo, which operates daily from 7 a.m. to 6 p.m., but note that it closes for lunch from noon to 2 p.m. Adjacent to the market, a small supermarket offers a selection of dry goods and essential items.

Accommodations in Puerto Villamil

The range of accommodations in Puerto Villamil is narrower than that in Puerto Ayora, offering options that cater to various budgets, from economical to luxurious. For those seeking to spend under $40 for two, expect compromises on aspects like air conditioning, location, or overall maintenance. Mid-range options priced between $50 and $100 boast numerous clean, spacious rooms conveniently located in the heart of town. If your budget exceeds $200, you'll discover several luxurious establishments with stunning views willing to accommodate your desires.

Budget-Friendly Stays Under $50

For budget-conscious travelers, **Posada del Caminante** is the most economical option, located about a 15-minute walk inland from Cormorán (tel. 5/252-9407, posadadelcaminante.com, $18 for single, $36 for double, no breakfast). While the fan-only rooms are basic, it features a shared kitchen, making it suitable for cooking, and is conveniently near the municipal market. The hotel has two sections: the main building and an annex across the street, with the upper-level rooms of the secondary wing (Posada del Caminante II) providing better value.

Hospedaje Sarita (located at Pepinos at Gil, tel. 5/301-6769, hospedaje.sarita@gmail.com, $30 for double with fan, $50 for suite with air conditioning and kitchen, no breakfast) is a superior choice for those looking to prepare meals. All rooms are straightforward and equipped with either an en-suite mini-kitchen or access to a shared kitchen. The suite, complete with a private kitchen and air conditioning, offers great value, and its location is more favorable than that of Posada del Caminante, being closer to the beach, Concha de Perla, and the town's central square.

If cooking isn't on your agenda, **Hospedaje Mother Fanny** (located at Gil at Escalesias, tel. 97/997-9678, hospedajemotherfanny@yahoo.com, $25 for single, $40 for double, no breakfast) provides affordable air-conditioned doubles in a central location. While the rooms are modest, they are ideally situated right in the heart of town.

For a budget-friendly option with more appealing rooms, consider **Casa Sea Lions** (at Fragatas and 16 de Marzo, tel. 5/252-9198, hotelgrantortuga.com, $30 for single, $50 for double, no breakfast), which is managed by the adjacent Hostal Gran Tortuga. Casa Sea Lions features bright, cheerful rooms on the second floor and enjoys a prime location.

The best economical lodging directly on the beach is **Casa Soleil** (located at Conocarpus at Malecón, tel. 9/940-3069 or 5/252-9121, oseegers@gmx.de, $40-45 for single, $50-60 for double, breakfast available for $5). This family-run establishment has three basic rooms, with the upstairs room being the most desirable and worth the extra cost. Direct bookings are encouraged for the best rates.

Mid-Range Accommodations Between $50 and $100

In the mid-range price bracket, all hotels provide air conditioning, hot water, Wi-Fi, and breakfast included. A reliable choice is **Gran Tortuga** (at Fragatas and 16 de Marzo, tel. 5/252-9198, hotelgrantortuga.com, $45 for single, $67 for double, $105 for triple), a small hostel known for its friendly service and cheerful rooms furnished with large, firm beds. The doubles on the second floor represent good value, and guests can relax on the third-floor terrace adorned with hammocks.

Another dependable option is **Rincón de George** (located at 16 de Marzo and Gil, tel. 5/252-9214, rincondegeorge@gmail.com, $55 for single, $70 for double, $105 for triple). The guest rooms are comfortably furnished and include firm beds, hot water, and TV. The owner is a licensed tour guide, and a continental breakfast is served on the fourth-floor terrace, complemented by a communal kitchen.

For those venturing farther inland, **Gran Hostal Tintorera** (located at Escalesias at Cormoran, tel. 5/252-9248, Galápagostintorera.com, $40 for single, $70 for double) offers slightly larger rooms in a serene courtyard filled with fruit trees and hammocks, although it requires an additional four-block walk from the main attractions.

Hotel Cally (located at Gil at Piquero, tel. 5/252-9072, hotelcallygalapagos.com, $60 for single, $90 for double, $140 for triple) is a medium-sized hotel boasting clean, spacious rooms in a new building, located conveniently near the beach and downtown, with noisier rooms available for $35 per person.

The charming Wooden House Lodge (at Gil, tel. 5/252-9235, thewoodenhouse.com.ec, $45 for single, $90 for double) is a delightful cabin-style lodge positioned on the east side of town, the closest lodging to the snorkeling site at Concha de Perla. Its cozy rooms feature wooden interiors, although the pool is less inviting. It's just a 10-minute walk into the heart of the town.

Caleta Iguana (located at Gil, tel. 5/252-9405, iguanacove.com, $30-100 for double), also known as Casa Rosada, includes a surf camp and tour agency, making it ideal for beachgoers. The accommodation options range from basic fan-only rooms facing the street for $30 (no breakfast) to ocean-view rooms with air conditioning and breakfast for $100. Despite some rooms showing signs of wear, the lively atmosphere and prime location make it a popular choice. The on-site bar is the town's favorite, adding to the vibrant social scene, though it can lead to noise at night.

Drake Inn (located at Gil, tel. 5/301-6986, drakeinngalapagos.com, $98-130 for double, $178 for a two-bedroom suite) stands out with its unique character and cheerful, breezy rooms featuring a nautical theme. Guests can enjoy views through port windows or relax in the aqua-colored lounge. The hotel offers two sunny terraces, allowing visitors to unwind in the sea-view Jacuzzi or from the third-floor terrace overlooking the beach and lagoons.

Luxury Stays Over $100

As Puerto Villamil expands its appeal to luxury land-based tours, several high-end accommodations have emerged. **Isabela Beach House** (located at Gil at Pepino, tel. 5/252-9303, theisabelabeachhouse@gmail.com, $132 for double, $160 for double with ocean view, $200 for triple) is a beachfront property run by an American expat that prides itself on its personalized service. The simple yet charming rooms feature beach-themed decor, with breakfast ($10 per person) served on tables right on the sand.

On the east side of town, you'll find the artistic **Casa Marita** (at Gil, tel. 5/252-9301, casamaritagalapagos.com, $115-125 for double, $170-220 for suites). This 20-room beach house showcases individually decorated rooms filled with eclectic art and furnishings curated by its Peruvian and Italian owners. Each room includes a mini-fridge, though there are no TVs. Instead, enjoy the sunsets from beachside lounge chairs and hammocks. The elegant upstairs restaurant features a menu of Italian, Peruvian, and Ecuadorian dishes. The more mundane extension wing across the street lacks ocean views.

Opened in 2017, **S Hotel Cormorant** (located at Av. Antonio Gil y Calle Los Pinguinos, tel. 5/252-9192, $160 for interior view, $180 for ocean view, $250 for suite) boasts stunning panoramic views of the ocean, complemented by polished wood and lava rock accents. The charming courtyard is adorned with painted blue-footed boobies and frigate birds on the polished concrete floors. Breakfast is served at the nearby Sun & Coffee restaurant, and while interior-view rooms lack the breathtaking vistas, the ocean view accommodations and suites are truly impressive.

Hotel Albemarle

Located right in the heart of town, Hotel Albemarle (Malecón, tel. 5/252-9489, www.hotelalbemarle.com) features 17 rooms, including 12 with breathtaking ocean views. Guests can enjoy a refreshing dip in the pool surrounded by tropical greenery. The accommodations are stylishly decorated with high ceilings and a modern coastal aesthetic, creating a serene atmosphere for relaxation.

Isamar

Isamar (Gil, tel. 593/99 555-3718, isamargalapagos.com/en/home) is an upscale lodge that boasts just eight spacious rooms located on a prime beachfront. The modern interiors are complemented by crisp white linens and security boxes for your peace of mind. Many rooms provide unobstructed views of Isabela's extensive sandy beach, while the deck is adorned with comfortable lounge chairs, perfect for soaking up the sun.

Iguana Crossing

Situated on the quiet west side of town, Iguana Crossing (Gil, tel. 5/252-9484, www.iguanacrossing.com.ec) offers luxurious accommodations with 14 elegant guest rooms featuring stylish decor, flat-screen TVs, and mini-fridges. Guests can indulge in stunning ocean views from their rooms. The hotel boasts a small pool deck with oversized lounge chair beds, and the third-floor terrace presents a spectacular panoramic view of both the beach and lagoons. The on-site restaurant serves a variety of gourmet local and international dishes, ensuring a delightful culinary experience.

Scalesia Lodge

For those seeking an unforgettable experience, Scalesia Lodge (tel. 593 3/2509504, www.scalesialodge.com) offers a luxurious glamping adventure in Isabela's lush highlands. Inspired by luxury safari camps in Africa, the lodge provides a unique camping experience that combines nature with comfort. Given the challenging access, most guests opt for all-inclusive packages or island-hopping adventures to make the most of their stay.

Puerto Villamil presents a diverse range of accommodations that cater to various budgets and preferences, from budget hostels to luxurious resorts. Whether you're looking for a simple place to lay your head or a lavish getaway with stunning views, you'll find plenty of options to enjoy the beauty of Isabela Island.

Essential Information and Services on Isabela Island

Isabela Island lacks banks and ATMs, so visitors are strongly encouraged to carry sufficient cash for their stay. While some upscale hotels may accept credit cards, having cash on hand will ensure a smooth experience.

For tourist-related inquiries, the local iTur tourist office is conveniently located at the corner of 16 de Marzo and Las Fragatas (tel. 5/301-6648), operating from 9 AM to 5 PM, Monday through Friday. The national park office is situated one block from the main plaza at the intersection of Gil and Piqueros (tel. 5/252-9178) and is open from 7 AM to 12:30 PM and 2 PM to 7 PM, Monday through Friday.

Accessing Isabela Island

General Villamil Airport (IBB) is located just north of town and provides a short taxi ride to reach it. This airport exclusively offers interisland flights connecting to San Cristóbal and Baltra; direct flights from mainland Ecuador to Isabela are not available. Small eight-seat planes operate on a half-hour schedule several times a week between San Cristóbal, Baltra, and Isabela, with one-way fares starting at $160 and round-trip fares at $240. Reservations for interisland flights can be made through Emetebe (tel./fax 5/252-0615, www.emetebe.com.ec) or FlyGalápagos (tel. 5/301-6579, www.flyGalápagos.net).

Interisland Ferries

Interisland ferries operate daily from the main dock, offering transportation to Puerto Ayora, which takes approximately 2 to 2.5 hours at a cost of $30 per person one way. Ferries leave Isabela at 6 AM and 3 PM, while the return trips depart Puerto Ayora at 7 AM and 2 PM. Although it's possible to arrive in Puerto Ayora in the morning and catch an afternoon ferry to San Cristóbal the same day, no direct routes are available. Upon landing, expect a $10 tax per person at the dock ($5 for Ecuadorian residents). Water taxis from the ferry to the dock charge $1 per person.

Local Transportation

Buses to the highlands operate just once daily in the early morning, and guided tours are necessary to visit the Sierra Negra volcano. For local exploration, taxis are readily available near the main plaza, charging $1 for short trips within town and $10 per hour for visits to nearby attractions. Renting bicycles is a popular option, with rates at $3 per hour, providing an excellent way to discover Los Humedales and the surrounding areas at your own pace.

AROUND PUERTO VILLAMIL

Attractions

Los Humedales and Centro de Crianza

Los Humedales, or The Wetlands, is home to the notable Wall of Tears, which serves as a poignant reminder of Isabela's history. This area also boasts beautiful beaches, scenic viewpoints, a tortoise breeding center, and numerous lagoons. Located six kilometers west of Puerto Villamil, visitors can embark on a half-day guided tour via van for $25 per person. For those seeking a full-day adventure, bike rentals are available at $3 per hour, or hiking is an option as the trail to the Wall of Tears is mostly flat along the beach. However, the final stretch to the Wall involves an uphill climb on a hot, exposed road. A popular choice is to take a taxi to the Wall of Tears for $5 and return on foot or by bike.

Before departing from Puerto Villamil, a visit to Laguna Salinas at the western end of town is worthwhile, as it sometimes attracts flamingos. Although the lagoon itself has limited attractions, its proximity to town makes it a quick stop.

Centro de Crianza (Tortoise Breeding Center)

Located 1.6 kilometers inland from the main road, the Centro de Crianza can be accessed by following the signs. A hiking trail parallels the main road and passes several lagoons where flamingos may be spotted. This breeding center houses around 850 tortoises distributed across eight enclosures, all from Isabela Island. An informative center provides insight into the life cycle of these unique creatures and highlights conservation efforts for the island's five tortoise subspecies. After visiting the breeding center, it's necessary to retrace your steps to continue exploring the sights in Los Humedales. Note that this facility is similar to the Charles Darwin Research Station on Santa Cruz and La Galapaguera on San Cristóbal; typically, visitors only need to visit one of these locations.

Lagoons and Beaches
At the western fringe of Puerto Villamil, a series of lagoons attract flamingos for mating. Poza de los Diablos, the largest lagoon in the Galápagos archipelago, features wooden walkways that guide visitors through the area before leading to a forest trail. The smaller Pozas Verdes are known for their greenish waters, bordered by cacti. Don't miss Poza Escondida, a hidden lagoon at the end of a short trail.

Playita, a tiny sandy cove, is easy to overlook. This charming spot features a narrow strip of sand, rocky areas with marine iguanas, and a tranquil sea view. Nearby, a forked path leads to Playa del Amor, a picturesque beach frequented by marine iguanas, while the right path leads to Túnel del Estero, where visitors can explore a rocky tunnel and enjoy ocean views.

The Camino de Tortuga, a brief trail flanked by lush majagua trees, leads to a peaceful mangrove-lined inlet, ideal for wading and cooling off.

Wall of Tears and Mirador Orchilla
From Playa del Amor, biking another 30 minutes uphill (or walking for an additional hour) brings you to the final two attractions in Los Humedales. Mirador Orchilla is a wooden staircase offering breathtaking panoramic views of the island. The Muro de las Lágrimas, or Wall of Tears, is a 100-meter-long (328 ft) and 7-meter-high wall with a harrowing history. Constructed by convicts from a penal colony in the 1940s, its sole purpose was punishment, which adds to the tragedy of those who suffered during its construction. A set of steps provides a vantage point to appreciate both the wall and the surrounding landscape. If you're fortunate, you may encounter wild giant tortoises that have been repatriated from the breeding center.

Snorkeling at Tintoreras Bay
Just off the dock at Puerto Villamil lies Tintoreras Bay, the premier snorkeling location in the area. This group of islets, named Las Tintoreras due to the reef sharks found nearby, is accessible via a small panga (dinghy) ride. During the ride, expect to see penguins, sea lions,

and blue-footed boobies. After a dry landing, a short trail leads through unique rocky terrain adorned with whitish-green lichens atop craggy black volcanic rocks. Along the trail, you may spot Sally Lightfoot crabs and nesting marine iguanas. At the trail's end, observe whitetipped sharks resting in a channel. The tour includes a snorkeling session in clear, shallow waters teeming with rays, sea lions, and various fish species. Day tours are priced at $40 per person.

Exploring Los Túneles
A 45-minute boat ride south of Puerto Villamil takes you to the stunning rock formations known as Los Túneles, also referred to as Cabo Rosa and El Finado. Here, boats navigate through rocky mazes where stone archways form the famous tunnels over the ocean. The tour includes a brief walk across rocky terrain, offering views of blue-footed boobies perched on endemic opuntia cactus trees while majestic sea turtles glide below. After the walk, snorkeling opportunities abound, with numerous sea turtles resting in the vicinity. Day tours to Los Túneles are available for $110 per person.

Visiting Isla Tortuga
Isla Tortuga, a crescent-shaped island about an hour by boat from the port, is renowned for its diving opportunities. Snorkeling tours are also available, aiming to spot Galápagos sharks, hammerheads, and manta rays that divers often encounter in the deeper waters at the cleaning station. However, be prepared for challenging currents. Some tours combine a visit to Isla Tortuga with a stop at Cuatro Hermanos, a more distant islet. Day tours cost $110 and may not be available every day.

Puerto Villamil, Isabela, Galápagos

ISABELA HIGHLANDS

The premier adventure from Puerto Villamil is the hike to the **Sierra Negra**, Isabela Island's oldest and most active volcano, with its last eruption occurring in 2005. The trek to the Sierra Negra and Volcán Chico offers breathtaking geological sights. The most common route takes hikers about an hour to reach the Sierra Negra crater, which measures an impressive 10 kilometers (6.2 miles) in diameter. After soaking in the views, hikers continue for approximately an hour and a half to **Volcán Chico**, a series of lava cones located northwest of the main crater. This side is less prone to mist and rain, providing stunning vistas over northern Isabela and the distant Fernandina Island. Expect the entire hike to take around five hours of brisk walking with minimal breaks, or opt for a shorter, more leisurely two-hour trek to the crater's edge and back.

Some tour operators enhance the experience by including stops at **Mirador de Mango**, which boasts a panoramic 360-degree view of the island, and the **Cuevas de Sucre**, a fascinating lava tunnel reminiscent of those found on Santa Cruz. Other tours combine the hike with lunch at **Campo Duro Ecolodge** and a visit to the tortoise reserve. For those seeking adrenaline, some excursions also offer the option of downhill biking back to town after the trek. Standard day tours to Sierra Negra and Volcán Chico are priced at $35 per person. Those who wish to include lunch and downhill biking should expect additional costs.

For adventurous souls looking for a more challenging experience, a trek to **the Las Minas de Azufre** (Sulfur Mines) is available, though it's significantly less popular. This demanding seven-hour hike, particularly treacherous during the rainy season due to muddy trails, culminates in a dramatic descent into the sulfur mines, where toxic gases are released (be sure to hold your breath!). Given the difficulty and unpopularity of this tour, it is typically offered only as a private experience. It is advisable to team up with other travelers to book through a tour agency, which can reduce costs. For a group of four, the price per person typically ranges from $90 to $100. Camping tours at the sulfur mines are also available but tend to be pricier and less frequently booked.

Nautilus Tours offers the Sierra Negra and Volcán Chico trek for $40 per person. For more information, visit their website at nautilustour.com or contact them at +5 252-9076.

NORTHERN AND WESTERN ISABELA ISLAND

The northern and western shores of Isabela Island boast some of its most remarkable attractions, accessible exclusively via cruise tours. Each site offers unique encounters with wildlife and stunning landscapes that define the Galápagos experience.

Punta Moreno serves as a welcoming point for vessels arriving from the south. Visitors reach this site through a panga ride along the impressive sea cliffs and into a mangrove grove, where they can spot great blue herons and penguins. A subsequent dry landing allows for a challenging 2-kilometer (1.2-mile) hike over pahoehoe lava, accompanied by cacti, leading to brackish ponds that attract flamingos and white-cheeked pintails during the right season. Hikers are rewarded with panoramic views of three of Isabela's towering volcanoes. It is recommended to wear sturdy shoes due to the rocky terrain and to carry ample water and sunblock for the demanding hike.

Elizabeth Bay, located north of Punta Moreno, lacks a landing site, so exploration here is limited to panga rides. Visitors may encounter sizable marine iguanas and flightless cormorants in the bay. These iguanas thrive on the abundant algae, contributing to their impressive size. Further exploration leads to shallow lagoons where rays, turtles, and occasionally white-tipped sharks can be observed. The journey continues to the rocky islets of **Las Marielas**, home to a small colony of nesting penguins.

Urbina Bay, formed by dramatic geological events in 1954, provides a unique glimpse into the island's volcanic history. Following a wet landing on the beach, guests can wander along a short loop trail that reveals coral littered with marine life bones and shells, creating an eerie yet fascinating landscape. This easy hike, taking less than two hours, is an excellent opportunity to spot land iguanas, giant tortoises, and various bird species like blue-footed boobies and flightless cormorants. The bay is also home to rays and sea turtles.

Tagus Cove showcases the imprint of human history, as the cliffs here are adorned with graffiti dating back to 1836, left by whalers and other visitors. The demanding 2-kilometer (1.2-mile) hike from the cove rewards hikers with breathtaking views over Darwin Lake, a deep, salt-laden crater lake formed by seawater intrusion through porous lava rock. The path leads to the lower slopes of Volcán Darwin, offering stunning vistas of Isabela Island. After the hike, a panga ride provides excellent snorkeling opportunities along the rocky northern shore, where marine life such as sea turtles, penguins, flightless cormorants, marine iguanas, and sea lions can be observed.

At Punta Vicente Roca, snorkelers can delight in the opportunity to swim with sea turtles in a serene cove at the base of Volcán Ecuador. This site is renowned for its rich marine biodiversity, including flightless cormorants, penguins, and a variety of fish. Following snorkeling, guests can enjoy a panga ride past striking cliffs and into a tuff cave, where fur seals are often spotted.

While these are the main highlights, Isabela Island is home to additional sites with limited access. Just north of Tagus Cove lies Punta Tortuga, a mangrove-fringed beach where the elusive mangrove finch can be spotted. At the northern tip of Isabela, Punta Albemarle features a former U.S. radar base from World War II, where visitors can observe flightless cormorants and penguins from the boat, despite the lack of a landing site.

On the eastern side of Isabela, Punta García is one of the few places to see flightless cormorants and marks the trailhead for Volcán Alcedo, which boasts a massive 7-kilometer-wide (4.3-mile) crater and is home to the largest population of wild giant tortoises in the islands. This species, endemic to Volcán Alcedo, represents the largest of the giant tortoises. Unfortunately, access to this site is currently restricted to scientists only, leaving tourists unable to explore this remarkable area.

FLOREANA

Floreana Island, the smallest of the inhabited Galápagos Islands, spans just 174 square kilometers (67 square miles) and is home to a mere 130 residents. Southern cruises often include a stop here, drawn by the serene mangrove-fringed coastline and unique attractions such as the eccentric post barrel, where visitors can send postcards. Snorkeling opportunities abound in the nearby islets, making Floreana a popular destination for day tours that reveal the island's enigmatic history.

Visitors are treated to opportunities to relax on black-sand beaches, swim alongside sea turtles, and immerse themselves in the slow-paced Galápagos lifestyle. Those considering an overnight stay should come prepared, as food options are scarce and there are no banking facilities or ATMs. Additionally, insect repellent is essential due to the island's notorious mosquito population.

Key highlights of Floreana include the stunning beaches of Playa Negra and La Lobería, the tranquil mangrove-lined shores of Mirador de la Baronesa, and exceptional snorkeling locations at the submerged volcanic cone of Devil's Crown, along with the nearby Enderby and Champion Islands.

Stone sculpture on the island of Floreana

PUERTO VELASCO IBARRA

Puerto Velasco Ibarra offers a glimpse into a simpler way of life, where residents navigate dirt roads at a leisurely pace, exchanging warm greetings as they pass one another. This small town, unique in the Galápagos, prioritizes agriculture and fishing over tourism. It lacks banks, convenience stores, and cell phone coverage, with mail service limited to the iconic barrel at Post Office Bay.

Notable Attractions

Playa Negra, situated directly in front of Hotel Wittmer, welcomes both guests and the public alike. While it often hosts tour groups in the afternoons, the beach can be remarkably tranquil at other times, allowing for peaceful sunbathing. Swimming and snorkeling are enjoyable here, although the marine life is not as abundant as that found at the nearby La Lobería.

La Lobería is a must-visit for snorkelers, as it boasts a small colony of sea lions and a rich population of marine turtles that frequent the area to feed.

Visitors can embark on a scenic 900-meter (2,950-foot) walking path from the town, which winds through black lava formations and cactus forests, offering beautiful ocean views and a prime sunset spot.

Tour Options

Day tours from Puerto Ayora to Floreana typically cost around $80, but the lengthy transit time makes this option less appealing, as the boat journey takes about two hours each way. These tours include stops at Asilo de la Paz, the tortoise reserve, Playa Negra, and La Lobería. As tourism on Floreana is still developing, there are no dive operators or resident naturalist guides. For those staying on the island, many attractions are accessible independently, or you can join a day trip for about $20 by arriving at the dock around 10 a.m.

For other activities, booking through CECFLOR (Centro Comunitario Floreana) is necessary, as they are the only tour operator on the island. You can reach them at tel. 5/253-5055 or reservas.postofficetours@gmail.com. Keep in mind that tours require a minimum of four participants and may not operate daily. While specific prices for these tours are not yet established, options include:

A guided hike to Post Office Bay and Mirador de la Baronesa, which lasts three hours and includes snorkeling and a speedboat return to port. _Note that walking independently from the port is prohibited and can incur hefty fines._

A kayaking excursion to Post Office Bay and Mirador de la Baronesa, requiring a moderate fitness level, with each leg taking approximately 1.5 to 1.75 hours.

Kayak rentals for exploring the bay.
A kayaking trip to La Botella, an excellent snorkeling location, priced at $45 per person (with a two-person minimum). The kayak ride along the coast takes about 40 minutes each way.

Bicycle rentals are expected to be available soon, offering tours through the highlands and local farms. Future plans may include camping tours at Mirador de la Baronesa and excursions to Devil's Crown, currently only accessible via cruise.

Dining Options
Day tour packages generally include lunch, but for independent travelers, food choices are limited. All restaurants in the area are casual and feature outdoor seating, with no upscale dining options available. Meal times can be unpredictable, as many establishments will not prepare food unless customers are present; therefore, notifying a restaurant of your visit two hours in advance is advisable. Standard prices are $7 for breakfast, $12 for lunch, and $15 for dinner.

The Canchalagua (12 de Febrero) is the only coffee shop and café in town, known for its friendly service and homemade dishes, particularly the canchalagua pizza and burgers made with local mollusk.

The Devil's Crown Bar-Restaurant (12 de Febrero) serves breakfast, lunch, and dinner daily from a fixed menu, although the atmosphere is basic. Patrons often rave about the delicious fried fish served here.

Located at the end of the main road, **Oasis de la Baronesa** (12 de Febrero, tel. 5/253-5006) offers lunch and dinner options featuring typical fare like fish, rice, and a small salad, along with a starter soup.

For a popular choice among tour groups, **Leila's Restaurant** (Juan Salgado, tel. 5/253-5041) provides breakfast and lunch daily. The menu mirrors that of other establishments on the island, serving set meals of soup and rice accompanied by fish or chicken, all in a pleasant setting with long wooden tables, greenery, and hammocks.

Accommodations on Floreana Island

Puerto Velasco Ibarra offers a few distinct lodging options with a rich sense of history. Both Black Beach House and Hotel Wittmer are managed by descendants of the Wittmer family, early settlers in the Galápagos whose experiences are chronicled in various books and a documentary. Hotel Wittmer and Floreana Lava Lodge primarily accommodate larger tour groups.

Black Beach House is situated right on Playa Negra and can be reached at 5/252-0648 or 98/475-5473 (ingridgarciawittmer@hotmail.com, $30 per person). This two-room brick house features a spacious living area that overlooks the beach and is equipped with hammocks outside. A fully stocked kitchen allows guests to prepare meals, which is advantageous as dining out on Floreana tends to be pricier and less convenient than on other islands. For those interested in cooking, it's best to buy supplies from Santa Cruz.

Hotel Wittmer, located on Playa Negra and reachable at 5/253-5033 (erikagarciawittmer@hotmail.com, $30 per person), is notable for its historical ambiance, featuring a small exhibition about the Wittmer family's legacy in the sitting area. Guests can enjoy stunning views from the second-floor rooms. The accommodations are basic yet comfortable, with amenities like hot water and ceiling fans; some rooms also come with mini-fridges. Valuables can be stored in a safe-deposit box since there are no room keys. This hostal mainly serves organized tour groups.

The Floreana Lava Lodge, located on the road to La Lobería, is the island's priciest option (tel. 5/253-5022, malourdes.soria@hotmail.com, $138 single, $153 double or triple, breakfast included). It consists of ten oceanfront cabins, providing a serene setting away from the town and stunning ocean views. The lodge offers air-conditioned rooms equipped with reading lamps, hairdryers, and safe-deposit boxes; triples feature bunk beds. Organized tour groups predominantly fill this lodge, and guests on all-inclusive packages can access the kayaks and stand-up paddleboards available on-site.

Community Tourism Guesthouses

In addition to conventional hostels, Floreana has seven guesthouses associated with a community tourism initiative. Each guesthouse charges $35 per person, though the quality and amenities can vary significantly. Here's a list of the best options, presented in order of quality. These guesthouses typically do not include breakfast or air conditioning. There are plans for further investment and renovations, which may lead to price adjustments.

All guesthouses require direct email reservations, as they do not use online booking platforms. You can also reach out to CECFLOR for specific requests regarding your preferred guesthouse.

1. Casa Santa Maria (Ignacio Hernández, tel. 5/253-5022, malourdes.soria@hotmail.com, $35 per person) is managed by the owners of the Floreana Lava Lodge. This guesthouse features six modern rooms equipped with mini-fridges, safe-deposit boxes, and hot water; it's located a block inland. Opt for a room on the third floor for a better experience.

2. Casa de Emperatriz (12 de Febrero, tel. 5/253-5014, orquideasalgado@hotmail.com, $35 per person) offers three less-than-ideal rooms a few blocks inland near the main road but stands out as the only budget-friendly option on the island with air conditioning. Some rooms come with mini-fridges.

3. Casa de Lelia (Ignacio Hernández and Oswaldo Rosero, tel. 5/253-5041, leliaflorimarc8@gmail.com, $35 per person) is located a block inland and provides comfortable rooms with updated bathrooms, hammocks, and hot water. Certain rooms also include mini-fridges.

4. Los Cactus (Oswaldo and La Baronesa, tel. 5/253-5011, loscactus.gps@gmail.com, $35 per person) is slightly inland near the dock and offers four basic, modern-style guest rooms. Two second-floor rooms have limited bay views. Guests can use a kitchen, though it's advisable to inquire beforehand.

5. Casa El Pajas (Wittmer at Zavala, tel. 5/253-5002, hospedaje.elpajas@gmail.com, $35 per person) features a charming tiki-style log cabin aesthetic, although it's further inland than other options. It includes a breezy second-floor sitting area and a couple of hammocks.

6. Cabañas Leocarpus (12 de Febrero, tel. 5/253-5054, veritoemi2006@gmail.com, $35 per person) offers a rustic ambiance, with second-floor guest rooms providing a distant view of the sea. Each room contains a double bed and a single bed.

7. Casa de Huéspedes Hildita (12 de Febrero and Juan Salgado, tel. 5/253-5079, $35 per person) includes five guest rooms arranged around an empty gravel courtyard. Note that this hostel enforces strict water usage policies, reflecting the island's scarcity of this precious resource.

Information and Services on Floreana

Services on Floreana are limited. Visitors should bring sufficient cash, as there are no ATMs or banks on the island. It's also advisable to carry clean clothes since there is no laundromat.

Food and snack options are scarce; the lone minimarket is often closed. For light snacks, there is a small bakery (panadería) near the power station at the east side of town, where you can buy loaves of bread, rolls, and soft drinks. If you're staying overnight, it's wise to bring snacks from Puerto Ayora. Certain food items, including fruits and vegetables without seeds (such as apples, bananas, pineapples, and pears), are permitted for entry.

Tap water can be consumed if boiled first, although many hostels offer large dispensers of drinking water.

The CECFLOR office, located by the main dock, is the island's only tourist information source. Like most local businesses, it operates in the morning until late afternoon, although hours can be erratic.

While there is no hospital on the island, a small medical clinic along the main road caters to minor injuries.

For internet access, there are no Internet cafés or phone booths for international calls. However, a free public Wi-Fi network is available that covers much of the town.

Traveling to and Around Floreana Island

Interisland Ferries

Floreana lacks an airport, making access available solely via cruise or speedboat from Puerto Ayora on Santa Cruz. Ferries operate on a limited schedule, so it's essential to verify the ferry timetable before making arrangements or booking accommodations. Ferries cost $30 and typically depart Puerto Ayora at 8 AM, arriving around 10 AM. The return journey leaves Floreana around 2:30 PM, arriving back at Santa Cruz by 4:30 PM.

Occasionally, organized island-hopping tour groups may charter speedboats directly between Floreana and Isabela or San Cristóbal, although public ferries do not operate these routes. Should you encounter such a group, you might inquire with the captain or guide to see if you can secure a spot, but do not rely on this possibility as many prefer to keep their tours private.

Getting Around Puerto Velasco Ibarra

Unlike other ports, Puerto Velasco Ibarra lacks taxis due to its small size. The only public transportation available is the local chiva, a rustic open-air bus that operates twice daily at 6 AM and 3 PM. This bus departs from the main road (12 de Febrero) and travels to the highlands, making stops at local farms to drop off residents and at Asilo de la Paz for tourists if needed. The journey lasts about an hour and a half before returning to port.

HIGHLANDS OF FLOREANA

Situated inland from the dry coastal area of Velasco Ibarra, the highlands of Floreana offer a vibrant contrast, characterized by lush greenery and diverse wildlife.

Attractions

Asilo de la Paz

A short journey of 8 kilometers (5 miles) from the port leads you to Asilo de la Paz, a captivating visitor site within the national park. Here, you can explore a tortoise reserve, a freshwater spring, and historical pirate caves, all connected by a clearly marked pathway. The tortoise reserve allows visitors to walk among these majestic creatures on a dirt path; unlike reserves on other islands, there is no breeding center here, as these tortoises were once pets of the island's residents before being relocated for conservation. Continuing along the path, you'll discover a modest freshwater spring, which, despite its size, holds historical significance as it once provided water for the entire island. Nearby, you'll find a stone carving of a face created by the Wittmer family children, echoing the moai of Easter Island. The adventure culminates at the pirate caves, carved centuries ago, which served as shelters for both pirates and the Wittmer family, the island's first settlers. While no artifacts remain, exploring these caves sparks the imagination.

Visiting Asilo de la Paz is often included in organized day tours, but you can also venture there independently. The chiva, an open-air bus, departs at 6 a.m. for just $1 and takes about 45 minutes to reach the highlands. It returns to the port after 90 minutes, allowing for a quick visit. However, for a more relaxed experience, consider taking the chiva to Asilo de la Paz and walking back downhill along the 8-kilometer path, stopping to admire Cerro Alieri along the way. Note that a second chiva leaves at 3 p.m., but it's advisable to avoid this option as the return trip could leave you walking back in the dark. If you are feeling adventurous, you can hike the entire 16-kilometer (10-mile) round trip, but be prepared for an uphill challenge. The trail can be steep, and Floreana's unpredictable weather means it's wise to carry a jacket and wear sturdy walking shoes.

Cerro Alieri

Cerro Alieri, located approximately halfway between town and Asilo de la Paz, offers another splendid opportunity for exploration. The trailhead is marked clearly on the left side of the main road leading to Asilo de la Paz. The hike to the summit involves a steep ascent along a well-maintained path and staircase, taking about 20 minutes to complete. At the top, you will be rewarded with stunning panoramic views of the island, including sights of Puerto Velasco Ibarra and Post Office Bay juxtaposed against the lush highlands. Birdwatchers may also spot Darwin's finches along the trail.

The walk from town to the Cerro Alieri trailhead is straightforward and takes about an hour each way. Alternatively, you can opt for the 6 a.m. or 3 p.m. chiva for $1, requesting to be dropped off at the trailhead and picked up later. Another option is to visit Asilo de la Paz first, then hike down to Cerro Alieri (a 1.5-hour walk) before returning to town, which takes about an hour.

mossy forest in floreana island galapagos

SURROUNDING ISLETS

The coastline and surrounding islets of Floreana boast some of the finest snorkeling locations in the Galápagos. Accessible day trips from Puerto Velasco Ibarra include La Botella, Post Office Bay, and Mirador de la Baronesa, while other sites are reachable exclusively by cruise.

La Botella

Located just past La Lobería, La Botella is a protected bay that offers excellent snorkeling opportunities. Here, you can encounter marine turtles, various fish species, and occasionally rays. This area is significantly more vibrant than La Lobería, with a rich underwater ecosystem. The beach at La Botella serves as a nesting ground for sea turtles. However, accessing this site requires a kayak tour, as there are no direct trails leading there from the port.

Post Office Bay

Post Office Bay stands out as one of the most unique destinations in the Galápagos, known for its quirky history. Established in 1793, this site began as a place for whalers to leave mail in a barrel for ships headed home, fostering a spirit of camaraderie among seafarers. Today, visitors can engage in this tradition by leaving postcards for fellow travelers and taking one home to deliver personally, although paying postage might be more practical.

A wet landing takes you onto the brown-sand beach, where you'll find the famous barrel-turned-box and remnants of a lava tunnel just a few meters away. To reach the tunnel, you may need to wade through water. Nearby, you can also explore the rusting remnants of a 1920s Norwegian fishing operation and enjoy a game of football with the local crews, if they invite you. However, be cautious of the introduced wasp population, as their stings can be quite painful. A scenic end to your visit includes a panga ride past a lively sea lion colony, where you might also spot sea turtles and even penguins.

Mirador de la Baronesa

Mirador de la Baronesa, or Baroness's Lookout, was once a favorite spot for the island's baroness to watch for passing ships. Today, this picturesque location, surrounded by mangroves, serves as a stopping point for cruise ships, offering snorkeling, kayaking, or panga rides to observe blue-footed boobies, sea lions, and the occasional penguin along the rocky shores lined with black lava and endemic cacti.

Punta Cormorant

Located on Floreana's northern coast, Punta Cormorant begins with a wet landing on a beach tinted green by olivine minerals. A 720-meter (2,362-foot) trail leads to a saltwater lagoon, where you can admire the island's lush surroundings. This lagoon is an excellent spot for observing flamingos and other wading birds, such as white-cheeked pintails and stilts. The area is bordered by palo santo trees, offering shelter to various bird species, including yellow warblers and flycatchers. Beyond the lagoon lies a stunning beach, known as "Flour Beach" for its exceptionally fine white sand, where you might see stingrays and spotted eagle rays. Sea turtles often nest on this beach from November to February, and while signs indicate restricted areas, you might still catch a glimpse of them swimming nearby. Note that snorkeling and swimming are prohibited in this area. Interestingly, despite its name, there are no flightless cormorants at this site.

Diving excursions to Punta Cormorant are available through day trips from Puerto Ayora on Santa Cruz Island, with prices reaching up to $200 per person for two dives.

Devil's Crown

Devil's Crown (Corona del Diablo) is a submerged volcanic cone located off the coast of Post Office Bay. Its jagged peaks rise above the water, creating a unique marine environment ideal for snorkeling. The site features numerous nooks and crannies that attract a variety of tropical fish, including parrot fish, angelfish, and damselfish, with the occasional sighting of sea lions and sharks. Be mindful of strong currents on the ocean side, and ensure you follow your guide's instructions. Access to this area is currently limited to cruise tours.

Enderby and Champion Islands

Enderby and Champion Islands are favored by snorkelers and divers alike. Enderby features an eroded tuff cone where you can swim alongside playful sea lions, while Champion Island, a small offshore crater, serves as a nesting ground for boobies. Although landing is prohibited on these islands, both sites offer excellent snorkeling and diving opportunities, with chances to encounter diverse shark species, colorful fish, and sea turtles. Like Devil's Crown, snorkeling at Enderby and Champion Islands is currently accessible only via cruise, while diving trips can be arranged from Puerto Ayora for about $200 per person for two dives.

SCAN THE QR CODE BELOW TO GET THE BONUS.

SCAN QR CODE

1. Open your phone's camera.
2. Aim at the QR code.
3. Wait for it to be recognized.
4. Tap if you need to scan.
5. Type 0$ under the (Name a fair-priced) search bar.
6. Click, I want this.

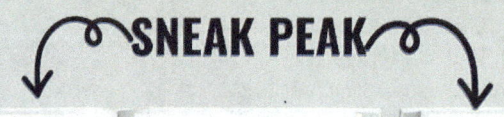

SNEAK PEAK

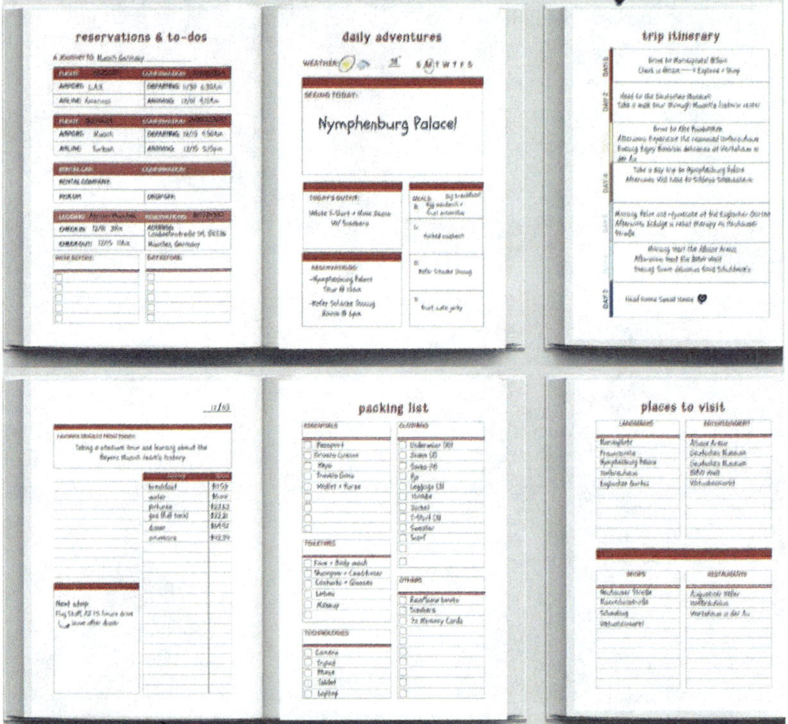

Page 94

GALÁPAGOS ISLANDS

SCAN QR CODE

1. Open your phone's camera.
2. Aim at the QR code.
3. Wait for it to be recognized.
4. Tap if needed to scan.
5. Follow the action prompted.

Made in the USA
Las Vegas, NV
14 March 2025